TIMEKEEPER

MY LIFE IN RHYTHM by

HOWARD GRIMES

with PRESTON LAUTERBACH

Devault Graves Books, Memphis

DEVAULT
GRAVES
BOOKS

THE GREAT MUSIC BOOK SERIES

Print Edition ISBN: 978-1-942531-40-1

Ebook Edition ISBN: 978-1-942531-41-8

Cover design: Kerri Mahoney

Layout design: Patrick Alley

Cover photograph: Michael Kerr

**DEVAULT
GRAVES
BOOKS**

INTRODUCTION
by Preston Lauterbach

My life as a writer began in a funeral home. This happened in July of 2006. I'd begun researching black Memphis music history with no specific goal in mind. I read an obituary in the paper for a man named Irvin Reason. He seemed like the sort of person I should get to know, to learn from—a saxophonist who'd played in the house band at Club Paradise and recorded with Bobby "Blue" Bland. Clearly I'd been too late. Finding a way to meet interesting people *before* they die would determine how satisfying my research could be.

I'd bought a book by Memphis musician Edward "Prince Gabe" Kirby called *From Africa to Beale Street*. In it, Prince Gabe lists alphabetically musicians who'd played on Beale. I got out my Memphis white pages and began searching for names from Prince Gabe's directory in the phone book. The first hit came right away on letter A: Able, Emerson.

On the phone, I told Mr. Able how Mr. Reason's obit had prompted me to call, and he said he'd planned on going to the visitation. He invited me to meet him there.

As I remember, the funeral home looked to me like it had been a car dealership in a previous life. The address on Elvis Presley Boulevard put it not far from Graceland, but the King had nothing to do with what happened that day. I sat in the lobby with Mr. Able and four or five other older guys on two sofas that faced each other.

I said little or nothing but listened.

The fact gradually dawned on me that one of the men, Ben Cauley, had played trumpet with the original Bar-Kays and survived the plane crash that killed Otis Redding and most of his bandmates in 1967. Another had been a songwriter at Stax and Hi, the two major Memphis soul record companies. Still another had played in joints around the city sixty years before. They teased each other, told stories about the deceased, and kidded Mr. Able for kicking Isaac Hayes out of the band at Manassas High School. Other old heads filtered in and out and stood by visiting with the guys in the lobby.

I learned that Mr. Able had played an unsung role in shaping a generation of the artists who'd made the Memphis sound. Other than Isaac Hayes, of course, though I guess he had his impact there in a way. Mr. Able told me how he'd grown up in North Memphis hearing about the great Jimmie Lunceford, who'd directed the Manassas High School band before leaving with its rhythm section to become one of the top orchestra leaders in swing. Artists like Frank Strozier, Hank Crawford, Harold Mabern, George Coleman, Booker Little, and Charles Lloyd had all started out in the Manassas band before moving to greater heights.

After an hour or so in the lobby, Mr. Able and I walked into the viewing room and took a quick look at Irv. We circled back out, and Mr. Able guided me towards the exit. "Bye, bye, Preston," he said. I kept going.

I figured he'd tired of me one way or another and that I may not get another chance to speak with him. I went home but later called Mr. Able to thank him for putting up with me. Far from brushing me off, he made the connection that changed my life. He said, "There's somebody I want you to get in touch with. He's been in the dark a long time. Student of mine named Howard Grimes."

Of course, I'd heard Howard, many times, without knowing, but I hadn't heard *of* him. That's Howard's way and his fate.

Mr. Able spoke of how he and the elder musicians had selected

Howard for a special role. "We trained Howard. We took him because we knew he's the only one who would tell the truth. Howard never talked, never ran his mouth, he listened and learned."

I understood just how rare these attributes are in a musician. So many of them are such born self-promoters, gifted storytellers, entertainers, and shape shifters, that the truth can have little to do with the historical interview.

Howard is but one of those things—a gifted storyteller. I came to realize that pretty quickly after meeting him.

Howard should be known for laying down the rhythm on Al Green records. Those rhythms come out so gently in such a relaxed and steady way, they resonate like a healthy heartbeat. Howard's rhythm has a therapeutic effect, as if the beat reminds you how you should be—how to breathe right, how to pace yourself, how to be laid back. As I got to know Howard, I felt that those rhythms are who he is. Listening to him speak, he delivers his words steadily, rhythmically, but with the flourishes and fills that only a great artist can add without skipping the beat. His voice had a semi-hypnotic effect on me. I felt a sense of euphoria around him that only comes from those at peace.

The more I listened to Howard, the more I knew that Mr. Able was right. Howard had become a trusted keeper of Memphis music history. From his start in nightclubs in the 1950s, to his work in the top studios of the soul era, he had sat and kept his mouth shut, and his ears and mind open. As a drummer, he absorbs the sounds of other musicians in order to set the right tempo. He is a keen and clear-minded observer. These traits make him a great historian. They allow him to take in other people's words and other people's mannerisms. He can bring the dead back to life if only for a moment, barking out the key like Rufus Thomas in an Orange Mound café, or jittering nervously like Sunbeam Mitchell used to. Howard can embody the lost characters of history.

From that moment of meeting Mr. Able, I found work as a

journalist and from there have written four books that touch on Memphis music, history, and culture. Mr. Able was a turning point for me. When I met him, I had no job and no clear path for my research or life. After I met him, people started seeing value in the stories I wanted to tell—stories he tipped me to or participated in as a source, about Jimmie Lunceford, the chitlin' circuit, Beale Street. I consider him a mentor just like he is to Howard Grimes. Maybe even more of a mentor than he was to Isaac Hayes. I think I've more or less done him justice. Mr. Able wanted the truth to be told and the credit where it belonged.

Howard and I went to see Mr. Able in a nursing home in 2015. Mr. Able always came off gruffly cheerful and this time was no different. Lying in the bed, he said he was ready to get the fuck out of there. As Howard and I did just that, we talked about what Mr. Able meant. Howard said he must have been ready to go home. In the next day or so, we learned that Mr. Able had died. *Here* is where he was ready to get the fuck out of.

This book is in many ways a culmination of a mentor's vision. Mr. Able helped me become a writer, and he helped Howard become a musician and historian. It's like Mr. Able brought us together to carry out his mission with the tools he helped us assemble.

Thanks to Mr. Able's guidance, Howard knows Memphis as no one else does. What Howard has to say about it will teach you things you didn't know, and change the things you thought you knew. His perspective is firsthand.

Of course in any big story like Memphis music, you'll have stars and heroes. But to Howard, Isaac Hayes wasn't Black Moses, he was a classmate. Al Green wasn't the sexiest man alive, but a guy who stopped by to smoke reefer in the basement.

There is evenness to Howard's rhythm, temper, and telling of the tale. His steady beat is not God-given, as you'll see, but learned. The trials Howard has been through would have ruined virtually any other man's sanity and health. He can speak in the same breath of how a person screwed him over, and how that person is a genius. In writing as in music, Howard's gift to us is his rhythm.

This is my own attempt to explain just how special a person Howard is, how great a story he tells, and I'm falling short, I know I am. So, I suppose there's only one way to let you know. This is his story in his words.

CHAPTER ONE

The thing I'm proudest of is being on drums when the two great Memphis soul studios, Stax and Hi, came to life. Stax wasn't even Stax yet, the company was still called Satellite Records, when I cut Rufus and Carla Thomas singing "'Cause I Love You," in 1959. That was their first big hit. Before that, the company had done some good things, but it didn't become Stax until we brought the Memphis sound. Same thing at Hi; they cut great instrumentals on Bill Black and Ace Cannon before I came along, but once I joined, the group hit with Willie Mitchell's "Soul Serenade" in 1968. After that, Willie discovered Ann Peebles and Al Green and put many other artists in the charts.

My beat is the backbone of the Memphis sound. The rhythm of this city runs through my heart. This book isn't just *my* story. I'm connected to the music in this city. The old masters I played with, that I came up under, they told me to listen to them, to tell what's happened and remember. They told me to tell the truth for them after they've gone. They've almost all gone.

As the drummer, I sat in the corner and listened. That was my job. I stayed quiet but absorbed the music and the history going down around me. I worked with some giants and some others who haven't gotten the recognition, but should be known. Everyone knows Al Green, but not as many are aware of O.V. Wright. I backed both of them. People know Ann Peebles' "I Can't Stand the Rain," but not as many have heard Denise LaSalle's "Trapped By A Thing

Called Love." I recorded both of them.

I don't know exactly how many records that I played on have sold, but it's well into the millions with plenty gone gold and plenty of Grammys handed out to other artists. As the drummer, it wasn't my job to be out front; I needed to hang back. I don't have to be in the light. The world don't have to see me. I don't need glory. People bought the records. They already *feel* me. But now it's my turn to step forward and tell all I saw and heard.

At my age and in the shape I'm in, people ask me if I work out. I say yes, mostly mentally. Everyone's in a rush. Time moves so fast. Everyone's in a mood. My mental workout comes from being a drummer. The Lord brought it before me. He said, "You're a time-keeper." I never knew what He was saying. I always felt drawn to the beat in music and the rhythm in life. Willie Mitchell told me, "I put the clock on you. I wanted to see if you were on time. You were perfect. Right with the second hand."

I'm connected to time.

Memphis, Tennessee was a great city when I was born, August 22, 1941. We had police who worked the streets. Firemen who kept us safe. I thought everything was all right. Peaceful. The city stayed clean. People filled up the parks on weekends, cooking out and playing softball or singing gospel songs. In music, I came up when rock 'n' roll got started. With blues and jazz, I saw everything that went before. Music blossomed all around me.

My mama wasn't but sixteen years old when she had me. My mama was running with my Uncle Sammy. He was shooting dice. He looked after her, but she'd slip off from the house.

My mother gave birth to me at home. My Aunt Luvenia told me that I had sores all over my body as a baby. Doctors didn't expect me to live, but Aunt Luvenia cured me. She told me, "I took a stick of butter and a pat of lard. I rubbed that butter and lard over your body, greased it real good and gave you to God."

As a kid I had the name "Peaches," and I didn't like it. "Peaches" sounds like a punk. I stayed mad about that and said, "Don't call me that." Aunt Luvenia told me, "The reason I gave you that nickname, after the third day of butter and lard on your skin, all the sores had gone. You looked golden and shiny like a peach."

Miss Bessie and people in the neighborhood used to see me and say, "There my Peaches! Peachy Pie!" I hated when she said it. My cousin Bilbo and all of them for years kidded me, "Whatcha doin' Peachy Pie?" But Aunt Luvenia said, "We call you that because you're special."

I never saw my real father, I don't know who he is. My mama was going with him when he got called into the service. I wasn't here yet. I heard all of this later, from my Aunt Rena Mae. I always tried to trace my daddy down, but never found him. I believe that some of my mother's old friends know, but no one ever wanted to tell me. My mother would get angry when I asked her.

Leroy Grimes was the one who gave me his name. I was already born when he came out of the service during World War Two. At that time, my neighborhood was like the country, just dirt roads. I saw a soldier coming down the road towards my home, and didn't know who it was. When he got to my house, he came on up. I ran inside. He came through the gate, and my mother started jumping and hollering. He looked surprised to see me. But my auntie told me Leroy gave me his name to keep me from being a bastard. My mama and my auntie would go to the NCO club at Millington. That's how she met Leroy and that's how she met my natural father. I always called Leroy Grimes "Daddy."

Daddy used to read the *Reader's Digest*. He'd take walks around the block. He liked quiet and he did his thing. My mama, she'd come in raising hell in the morning with that whiskey in her. He'd be laying in the bed. He never bothered her about partying. I don't think they fought much and I know he didn't hit her. He took care of business in the bedroom. I had to leave; I didn't want to hear all that. She'd be a new woman the next morning, skipping around the kitchen singing. She'd have a hot breakfast on the table.

We stayed with my grandfather, Winston Threat. My grandfather wasn't about mumbo jumbo. He kept his mind on work, God, and being a Mason. He led our family. He kept up the house. Granddaddy worked at Baptist Hospital. He had it all together. Granddaddy had a duplex on Smith Street. He lived on one side and my mama and us lived on the other. He enlarged the house as our family grew.

My grandfather kept the radio tuned to WREC, never another station. He listened to the Lone Ranger and seldom missed the Grand Ole Opry. His favorite was Hank Williams: "Hey Good Lookin'," and "My Bucket's Got a Hole In It." Great stories and great songs. They grabbed my imagination.

My granddaddy and his lodge brothers never had a cross word, never had an argument. They'd sit around the fire at night talking, and I listened. They had peace and respect about them. My granddaddy taught me to read the Bible and watch the news. Later, once I got out on the road as a musician, he told me he wanted me to be a Mason. He said being a Mason could get me into places no one else could get into. He said, "It sets you separate from the world. It's about brotherly love." Being around such rightful people, I never worried about anything.

I had a great life because everybody was for me—family, friends, and neighbors. My grandfather's children and grandchildren were all around. My auntie had a big old house nearby and many of my relatives stayed there. My mother had plenty of friends; everyone loved my mother. They called her Sister Threat. She loved to go and listen to music.

On Saturdays, Mama fixed women's hair in the kitchen. In the summertime, we had no air conditioning, and it'd be hot. While

Mama did their hair I stood there and watched the women flap their skirts to keep cool. It made a passage between their legs and I stared at something white down there, must have been their panties. I had to be between four and five. My mama said, "Boy, get your mannish ass outta here." But the women said, "Leave that little boy alone."

My granddaddy put a white fence around the yard. I stood out front of the house, watching the women walk up the street with their shopping. When they passed my house I asked if I could feel their legs. They'd poke their leg through the fence and I'd rub it.

My mother had a girl named Essie Mae take care of me and my brothers. She brought her boyfriend Fly around. I'd watch them wrasslin' on the bed. He'd be laying on top of her. She screamed at me, but Fly said, "He got to learn what a man and a woman is for."

Clyde Burnett, we called him June Bug, and I were the best of friends. My cousins Bilbo and Junior tried to get us to fight. Bilbo said, "Peaches can whoop June Bug." Junior said, "Nah, June Bug could whoop Peaches." They were trying to instigate us, but we didn't fight. We were such close friends, never had an argument. His mother, Miss Ollie, brought us big donuts, and my mother brought us popcorn and bubble gum.

My life growing up wasn't all easy. I had a heart murmur as a little boy and had seizures. I blacked out at times. To treat me, a doctor cut open my skull in the front of my head. That operation left me with a knot on my head. My hair never came back where they cut into my scalp. That ordeal became a big part of who I am. It changed me, forced me to take charge of my own life.

Back in those days, our doctor would come to the house. I heard him tell my mama, "Howard can't get upset. You have to keep him calm. If you don't, you'll lose him." After that, I started learning how to limit my temper, because I was scared to die. People think I'm laid back now—I've had to control my mind for as long as I can remember.

As a young person, I started searching my body. Scared me one time, laying up in the bed, I heard my heart, doom-doom, doom-doom. I learned to practice circuit breathing. From then on I could control my heart, slow it down. It's in the rhythm.

CHAPTER TWO

My neighborhood—New Chicago in North Memphis—stood off from the rest of the city. The city dump sat on one side of New Chicago. On another side of it stood a sea wall around the Wolf River. Along the river ran the levee road, which passed a junkyard before you'd get back to Thomas Street. The tall smokestack and many buildings of the Firestone tire factory stood all around. Most of the neighborhood worked there or the Humko shortening factory. Now it's all closed down and empty.

I stayed on Smith Street, which crossed North Bellevue Boulevard, where all the neighborhood action took place. Up on the corner of Smith and Bellevue, a guy called Big Buddy ran a poolroom. Next door to the poolroom, my Uncle Chris had a café. Uncle Chris was a high roller. He was like a pimp. He had curly hair, had some Indian blood in him. He looked like Bobby Rush. He's just like the other high rollers, buying pussy. My auntie was a freckle-faced woman, light-skinned. She knew what he was doing.

Uncle Chris lived quite a while. In his late eighties, still driving his Chevrolet, he had a girlfriend in her thirties. I used to ask him, "Why do you drink gin and juice?" He said, "I drink a shot of it every morning and my dick stands up as strong as yours." He died at age ninety-five.

Down the corner from Uncle Chris's was Fat Man's Café. That's where B.B. King and Bobby "Blue" Bland would do Blue Monday. My mother and them would go. Next to Fat Man's was

Mr. Boyle's grocery store, and across the street Mr. Cleve had a barbeque place where you could get ribs and shoulders. He was only open on Friday and Saturday nights. Down from there stood Mr. Eli's club. Mr. Eli weighed almost 400 pounds. He opened the door on a summer day and played the box. I heard the greatest music coming out of there—Big Joe Turner, Little Richard, Ray Charles—and took it all in.

It was a fun neighborhood. Everyone loved the blues. There was Miss Bessie's club, on White Street, a block from Smith. That's where they were drinking Falstaff, Stag, and Goldcrest 51 beers. Mr. Ben, Miss Bessie's husband, ran his barbershop next door. This was about 1950, so I was eight or nine years old. Miss Bessie's club was a little red and white house. In the summertime, that's when I heard that good music. On the weekend that place was booming. She was always open. Miss Bessie and Mr. Ben were some of the nicest people. Their daughters were my dancing buddies. I can still dance, I ain't forgot nothing.

This lady used to come to Miss Bessie's café for her husband. Her name was Miss Lizzie, but we kids called her Mama Yaya. She'd come get her husband out of Miss Bessie's. She carried a hammer with her. Come with that hammer, when he's sitting up at the café. She didn't hit him with it, but he knew what it was for. She just brought it to get him up and moving. She said, "I'm a give you one!" He got too drunk and she'd just coach him on back home. She didn't want anything to happen to him and got him out of there before anything could. He'd go home, sleep it off, and be back the next weekend, and so would she.

When we used to laugh and yell to her, "Mama Yaya!" she'd snap back, "Go to hell!" One time she took a piss and she didn't give a shit. She went upside the building and hiked up her dress and it streamed right out. She got through, raised up, and dropped her dress, and said, "Y'all go to hell!" We died. She was good people, it was just all in the neighborhood.

We had so much. From Jackson Cookie Company you could smell the vanilla wafers when they baked them. The aroma went all through the neighborhood. There was F&L sundries store run by a white couple who welcomed us. The man who owned the place drove a black and white Buick. They put in a jukebox and a pinball machine, so we had something to do on the weekend. My buddies and I got around that jukebox and sang doo-wop. We'd feed that thing nickels and sing, eat ice cream, hang out with the girls.

Out in the street, guys were doing whatever it took to make money. That's the reason I stay to myself. Guys had time on them, had been in and out of jail, and just continued on doing what they'd gotten in trouble with when they got out. That was the only way to make big money. They had the cars. They had the women. They were all cool. They didn't want jobs. New Chicago was hot. They were selling corn whiskey. They sold regular whiskey on Sunday. The guy dressed all in white, lily white, looked like he worked in a bakery. That guy sold liquor. Fat Man got his stuff from him. The man in white made all kinds of rounds, but dressing like a baker kept him confidential. That's the way people had to make a living.

The men wore the drape suit with the watch chain hanging down. When I saw that Spike Lee movie with Denzel Washington, that took me back. My uncle Sammy had the drape coat, the chain, white pants. Uncle Sammy took me everywhere when I was a boy. Uncle Sammy took me to church on Sunday, and in the evening we went to the movies. I could tell by the way he dressed, the way he carried himself, it was all good. He was taken sick at a young age and died of sugar diabetes. He was a man—I guess he's where I got it from—just stand to himself. Minded his own business, did his own thing, worked for his own money. He did go and get in fights over gambling. He'd come downtown to the Red Barn and see Count Basie, Duke Ellington, the big time acts. My mother said she got many whoopin's from their daddy for going to the craps house with Sammy. They had more places to go and things were much cheaper.

It was about music and fun.

Today all of my old neighborhood is gone; the expressway came straight through our home.

Because of me, my mama never finished school. She started working for Uncle Chris at the café, bartending. Mama had eight children after me. Leroy Grimes just up and left one day. He ended up in Battle Creek, Michigan. He told me, "Son, go where you're called." That's good advice, though I wish he hadn't followed whatever called him away from us.

I kept myself straight, but occasionally had a little trouble. One evening my grandfather had gone out, I opened up his drawer and found his Mason ring. I put it on, put some tape on it to help it fit. I went out in the street and started profiling. Our neighbor Mr. Stewart said, "Peaches, where'd you get that ring? I bet that's your grandfather's and he don't know you got it." I said, "Yes sir, he don't know." Mr. Stewart said, "Boy don't you know if I come asking for a sign from him, proof that he's a Mason, and he don't got it, I could kill him." That scared me. I didn't want him to kill my grandfather, so I put back the ring. My grandfather never knew, God rest his soul, that I took that ring out.

Another time in my childhood, my mother sent me to Mr. Boyle's grocery to pick up food. I think he sent a bill later, so I never paid. Once he was loading up a sack of groceries, and I saw this pack of Dentyne chewing gum. I grabbed it and put it in my pocket. Mr. Boyle saw me. When I walked out of the store, I stuck all that gum in my mouth. I got home and my mama asked where I got the chewing gum. Mr. Boyle had called her and told her I slipped it into my pocket. I didn't know I'd done wrong.

I got two whoopin's from my mama in my life. She whipped me naked with a peach tree limb. That tore my ass up. I guess parents were abusive back then, but that whoopin' did me good. I'm honest. My teachers all told me not to lie and that's all I know.

Music had always moved my spirit and it was a matter of time before I got into drums. I remember a boy named Clarence Atkins took some tree limbs and made drum sticks. I heard him beating on a garbage can—sounding great. He played the cadence he picked up from Manassas High School. In the evening I could hear the Manassas marching band dropping bombs—sounded like they were calling to me.

By the time I had got to ten or eleven-years-old, I had started picking up hymns in church. I attended Antioch Missionary Baptist Church of New Chicago. That's where Rev. Johnson baptized me. Those songs come back to me, especially "What a Friend We Have In Jesus." The church had no drums, just piano or organ. The rhythm came from the floor. My ear got tuned to people rocking their feet. That sound blended in with the organ and the people singing. I heard through the floor. Soul came out of that floor. That's what carried the beat. Everything fit into the rhythm. All the song came up through the floor. Spirituality has been part of my journey all along. I wasn't always a student of scripture, but I've steady learned from the Bible and it remains my rock today.

After the church rhythms came to me, I had to get a drumstick in my hands. A fellow named John Murray showed me how to hold a drumstick. He used to go with my cousin. She worked at John Gaston Hospital, and Murray was a cab driver for Littlejohn's, a black taxi company. He'd come to see my cousin and had these sticks in his back pocket. I didn't know what they were. He told me he played drums in a nightclub on Beale. I asked how he used those sticks. He pulled them out of his back pocket and put them in my hand. He said, "I'll show you a little pattern. I want you to practice this. This will build up your wrist. The name of this pattern is the mama-daddy roll." He said, "You hit ma-ma, da-dee, left, left, right, right, faster and faster." He said, "Take your time, don't rush. You'll learn the coordination."

Next time he came to see my cousin, I showed him what I could do, and he said, "Now, alright, you got that." Next he showed me the footwork. That coordination hung me up a long time, but as it sunk in I realized I had rhythm. Something moved inside me. Something took control of me and said, "This is your right hand, this is your left hand, this is your foot." It all became clear in my mind even though they were all going at different things. I held on to that feeling. I had it and I knew I had it. It synched up with the way I breathed to ease my heart and clear my mind.

Once Murray showed me the basics, I wanted to play in a band. At age twelve I joined the drum and bugle corps at Paradise Park in the heart of New Chicago. A man named Rev. Brown organized the band. He ran a funeral home on the corner next to the barbershop. Me and my best buddy Shelly Owens played drums. Rev. Brown gave me a big white snare drum to play, and that made me feel like the leader of the drum corps. Those marching band rhythms influenced my later work on records.

Shelly and I walked over to Manassas High School one night, while the students were having their prom. We could hear the music and followed the sound. I peaked through the window and saw the school big band, the Rhythm Bombers playing. They wore blue and gold uniforms, and had music stands. They played the song "Blue Flame" as their theme when the curtain parted. I saw Mr. Onzie Horne directing, Ray Joiner playing drums. I walked up to the window and stood there. I listened to that band play. That stuff sounded so good. I said, "I want to come to this school and do this. One day, I'll put on that uniform."

CHAPTER THREE

The dream I had that night came true. I met my first musical mentor at school, the Manassas band director, Mr. Emerson Able. While working on this book, I went back and interviewed him, and this is what he told me about my early days in the Manassas band.

I didn't discover Howard, Howard discovered me. He came into the band. We had a little old boy on drums. He couldn't do shit. Goddamn. Howard was beating on a fifteen-inch snare drum like they used in 1776. But I knew one thing, he's a human metronome. Wherever he start the beat, that's where it's gonna end up.

Mr. Able was like my dad. He raised us musicians. Mr. Able exposed us to so much great music. In the Rhythm Bombers, he had us swinging, playing Dizzy Gillespie, "Salt Peanuts," and advanced stuff.

Mr. Able told me to play, "straight time, 4/4 on the bass and the backbeat." That was to hold the beat in place. I could always hold time. His lessons stayed with me. When I started professionally, that's all the groups wanted—hold that time and don't move. They don't want you to go take you a little something and come back, no, stay there. On time. Lock in and stay. Otherwise you carry the other musicians out of synch. No flipping sticks, no showcase drumming. Just keep it straight and simple. Easy to explain but hard to do. Most guys want to show out, but I always got more out of staying in rhythm and not moving. I could feel the impact on the rest of the band. That's the reason Willie Mitchell named me "Bulldog"—I clamp down.

The live music scene right in my neighborhood gave me plenty of inspiration and it influenced my sound. Before I started playing, Currie's Club Tropicana on Thomas Street—a mile from my home—used to bring in Hank Ballard and the Midnighters. That place would be so full. That's how the New Orleans beat got here to Memphis. Those drummers were so tight. When you listen to James Brown's band, that's what was going on. Five Royales, same beat. I wanted to learn that beat so bad. The style in Memphis is a little more laid back. We like that delayed backbeat on the 4/4.

Club Tropicana had every top-notch artist there. Going back to my mother's time, she saw all the big acts at Currie's, like Ray Charles. At that time it was called Johnny Currie's Beer Garden. I saw a whole lot of stuff go on in those types of places, and I just didn't like beer gardens. People would fight and get cut, clown out front. I didn't understand why a man would get drunk and whoop his old lady. There wasn't much shooting at that time, but they was cutting folks.

My cousin Inetta Jean Finley and her friends took me over to let me see the band at Currie's. I saw Basie, Ramsey Lewis, Bill Doggett in my early days, and later played there behind Solomon Burke, Garland Green, and Syl Johnson.

That first night, Mr. Currie said, "He's too young to be in here."

My cousin told him, "He plays drums, and I want him to see the band and watch the drummer."

Mr. Currie said that'd be alright as long as Inetta Jean and her girlfriends would be responsible for me. They set me on the side of the stage, and I watched the drummer, Ed Smith. I sat there and had a Coke, hamburger, and potato chips, and I watched how the drummer worked his feet. He was playing shuffles. I watched what he did with his hands. That shuffle style was the thing in Memphis. That's the beat people danced to.

When I saw what was going on, I liked it. Beer gardens didn't scare me so much anymore. That was a big help since I'd be playing gigs in joints at least five nights a week before long, for the next fifteen years.

The community gave so much support and uplift to young musicians. I don't see it out here today. The black high schools, Melrose, Douglass, Booker T. Washington, and Manassas, had parades on Main Street. The schools paraded for Christmas or Cotton Carnival. The best drummer from each school would be looking for the other top drummers where the parade began. Maurice White, who became famous with Earth, Wind & Fire, played drums in the Booker T. Washington band. He'd come up and battle against me during our warm-ups. We studied each other's moves, tried to see who had the fastest hands. The competition and the talent were always thick around Memphis drummers.

At the time Maurice White and me were doing our thing, the Flamingo Room, a nice club on Beale Street, held a "Little Jazz" festival every Sunday. WDIA, a great community radio station, hosted the show and deejay Nat D. Williams promoted it. The top musicians from the schools would come and play for a real adult audience. I saw the top people—dentists, doctors, lawyers, all the black elites. They loved Ray Charles and that type of sophisticated music, so that's what we gave them. Seeing the well-dressed and well-mannered professionals appreciate music helped me become a professional.

Being downtown, I went to Main Street where Dewey Phillips had a booth in the five and dime store. He played *all* the music. He had another guy who worked with him, wore a gorilla mask. They were on TV. Every day, I rushed home from school to see what they were gonna play. He pushed Carl Perkins' "Blue Suede Shoes." More than that, he played the great black artists, Sam Cooke, Chuck Berry, Little Richard. The first time I heard Elvis I thought it was Carl Perkins. Dewey didn't call his name, just said, "We got us a new one by a singer from down in Mississippi," and he put on "Heartbreak Hotel." Elvis could sing like nobody else. From there Memphis music started developing.

When I got started performing music live, my Uncle Chris managed the Rivermont Club at Lamar Avenue and Central Avenue in Memphis. My music teacher Mr. Able and the music teacher at Booker T. Washington, Mr. McDaniel, used to play at the Rivermont. Mr. Able brought me there to play with them, and there was a discussion. I was only twelve-years-old and didn't have any business being in there. The club owners weren't going to let me play.

Uncle Chris heard them talking about me, and he said, "That's my nephew. I'll look after him. Let him play."

Because of him, I got to play my first nightclub gig. Mama used to tell me Uncle Chris had power downtown.

Mr. Able played horn like Cannonball Adderley, and Mr. McDaniel played piano and sang ballads. They taught me to use brushes. Mr. McDaniel talked about Max Roach and how good he *swept* with those brushes. Mr. Able said sticks make too much noise and not to use them in a nice place. He said people don't want to holler at each other across the table.

Working with those gentlemen gave me so many gifts. Mr. McDaniel was older than Mr. Able, and he taught many youngsters who became pros starting with Mr. Able and on through Phineas Newborn Jr. to Booker T. Jones. He had two bad-ass drummers during my time, Maurice White and "Pistol" Allen, who ended up staff drummer at Motown. Those two professors taught me, "You play for the people, you don't lock in on yourself." They taught me to be a musician and a gentleman. I try to be the best of both. That was a joyful time for me. As a kid, I got encouragement and took home a little money. I heard people say, "Keep it up, you're going places." I wanted to see these places.

While working on this book, I had to ask Mr. Able to remind me about our gigging at the Rivermont. He said, "We worked there two or three nights a week. The best night was when Robert Mitchum came through while filming a movie. He had a pipe as big as a coffee cup, filled full of marijuana. He's crazy about Erskine Hawkins."

That high-class swing is the type of stuff we played, Hawkins's "Tuxedo Junction."

Most of the Memphis musicians knew each other, and Mr. Able started telling other cats about me. Not long after starting at the Rivermont with Mr. Able, I went out with a four-piece combo led by a piano player named Bob Talley that included Alfred Rudd on sax and Wilbur Steinberg on bass. Mr. Rudd and Steinberg did all the singing. Steinberg did Nat "King" Cole, plus all the standards, and Rudd sang blues.

Mr. Rudd became another mentor to me. I had the chance to interview him for this book, and he told me, "You were a baby when we took you out. Thing about you, you'd listen at what we older musicians had to say. Another thing that impressed me about you was, if we set the tempo right there, it stayed right there."

We worked exclusively at the Hi-Hat, down on South Third Street. A couple who were dance instructors at Arthur Murray studio ran the place. Mr. Rudd said, "There were three or four clubs down there past the bridge over Nonconnah Creek. The buildings are gone and so are all the wine bottles the musicians left behind there. After work at the Hi-Hat we'd come up to Beale Street, go to Club Handy and listen to those guys argue and play."

Mr. Rudd had a big old white Chrysler station wagon, and we'd ride up to Sunbeam Mitchell's Club Handy to watch John Murray—the guy who gave me my first sticks and lessons—Joe Dukes, or Odie Lee Howard. Sunbeam had bands working two shifts, 9-2 and 2-4. Two drummers. These were the drummers that brought me up. One night Joe Dukes took a drum solo and started doing his thing until I thought something was wrong with him. Jumping around, crashing the cymbals. Looked like he had a fit. I wasn't on to that yet. Joe Dukes played with Jack McDuff's quartet, but he came back home from time to time.

One night we saw Bill Tyus twirling his sticks. He kept time. But Mr. Rudd said, "That ain't about shit." I wondered what he was getting at. He looked at me and said, "A drummer has to make the people get out they seats and dance. Make the people dance. Women want to shake their ass." I started understanding that people can't move to a beat that's too fast. "Ain't nobody come to see that," Mr. Rudd said, and sure enough when we looked around the club, everybody had sat down.

When I started playing, drummers said, "You got it." It just came naturally, but the more I learned, the more I wanted to know, the more I wanted to hear different musicians. I was never looking at money. Older musicians told me it'd come and to appreciate what's happening.

I brought my little money home to my mother. Mama took a job at Firestone but needed every cent to raise all of my brothers and sisters. I worked another job, too. Mr. Chalmers Cullins ran theaters all over Memphis, including the Savoy where I worked. He had a live horror show one night with Frankenstein, the Mummy, and the Wolfman. My friend and me were up in the chicken coop, where they run the film. Place was packed. They dropped the lights. They had Frankenstein laid out on a table. When that electricity hit Frankenstein and he raised up, everybody cleared out. Me and my friend were laughing. People ran down the street.

I wasn't but fifteen years old, playing music, making money, laying off school. There was a girl in my neighborhood, Mary Alice. I used to go by and see her. My friend Shelly Owens was going with Mary Alice's sister Marguerite. A fellow called Poochie was going with Mary Alice. Poochie was just a pretty boy and Mary Alice didn't care that much about him. We were all real young. One day I went to Mary Alice's house with Shelly, and it got into something else. This was a one-time deal.

Four or five months later the word got out that Mary Alice was pregnant. People said it was mine. I said it was Poochie's. I said, if it ain't Poochie's, it's Shelly's.

"It" turned out to be "they"—Mary Alice had twins. After the babies were born, I got a chance to see them and I was happy. They were named Ann and Jan. There's one picture of me holding two of them in my arms. My mother was proud of those babies. She didn't much like me being a father, the age I was. She took a look and said they definitely belonged to me. We did a blood test to confirm that I'm their father.

Mary Alice's mother Ruth was a whiskey head and a hateful woman. She had been talking about leaving Memphis. She talked right over my head. I didn't understand why she was being that way. I made decent money playing music. I wanted to help with the girls.

One day I went past their house and found that they had gone. The house was empty. They just up and left. Nobody told me. That really messed me up, because I didn't think I'd ever see them anymore. I learned that the family had moved to Los Angeles.

I didn't see my daughters again until they were twelve-years-old. I didn't know until much later that Mary Alice didn't just give birth to twins—she had triplets. A wealthy family immediately adopted one of the babies. I still don't know what became of her. I was still a kid when those babies were born.

My close relationship with the Holy Spirit is up there with music as the driving forces of my life. I don't just pray to God. I converse with Him. The first time God spoke to me happened while I walked through the ballpark with my baseball gear. The workingmen, the real men in my neighborhood, would sit down, drink that Goldcrest 51 and that Falstaff beer, and watch the ballgames. That's what got me interested in baseball. That became my hobby after music. I played with the WDIA team for a while and later joined the Black Devils. As a pitcher, I threw shutouts.

Walking to the field to play with the Black Devils, I heard a voice call my name. I'd seen people going down the street, talking to themselves. I didn't want to be one of them. I was looking for the voice. He called to me three times.

"Howard."

I heard it but kept walking, looking around to see where it came from.

"Howard."

The next time He called to me, He said, "Have you ever thought about what you want to be in life?"

I wouldn't say anything cause I didn't want folks to think I'm crazy. I saw a drunk one time walk into a telephone pole, step aside and say, "Excuse me."

So, I said, "I want to be in the family of God's great drummers."

He didn't answer, but things went to happening. The right musicians embraced me and put me to work. I started making money. Once I got making a hundred a night I said, "Shoot, I'm rich."

I went through so much since then. But my good friend Darryl Carter, he used to write songs for Motown, Stax, and Hi, he said, "When I look at all the records you've cut, all the hits you made, all of the artists you worked with, I believe you are in the family of God's great drummers."

CHAPTER FOUR

Over the years of my life in music, I've known and worked
with some of the biggest and best artists we've had in this country.
Not only those I've recorded with, but artists I played behind on
stage like Marvin Gaye and Jackie Wilson, people you don't think
about being part of the Memphis sound. But maybe the biggest
star I ever played with was one of the first. He came up right in my
neighborhood and went to my school. I met Isaac Hayes at the end
of tenth grade.

Isaac and I had homeroom together and were both taking band
under Mr. Able. Isaac had an old silver alto horn, but always messed
around on piano. Mr. Able said, "Put the horn down. Get out." That's
the way Mr. Able would come at you. He told Isaac, "Go over there
to home economics and tell the teacher I sent you." Mr. Able wanted
Isaac to focus on one instrument. He didn't understand that Isaac
had so much sound in him. Of course nobody at that time knew.
Except maybe Isaac.

The home economics instructor, Mrs. Barbara Blake Jones, also
taught choir and had a piano in her classroom. She had the choir to
come in before she taught home economics. Mrs. Jones took Isaac
under her wing. She put him in the choir and taught him arranging
and keys. That's what made him who he was. Mr. Able helped Isaac
along by putting him out of the proper high school band and into
Mrs. Jones's class.

Isaac didn't forget that. Isaac had a peculiar way of getting revenge. When Isaac got big, he hired Mr. Able to be in his band, the Isaac Hayes Movement. Isaac went to bossing around the man who had kicked him out of the school band. They were cool, though, and Mr. Able appreciated Isaac for taking him out on the road.

Isaac used to sing with a girl named Laura who he later married. They used to do Brook Benton-Dinah Washington style duets at the school talent shows. That was the first time I started to see who Isaac was.

During my later years in high school, a man named Ben Branch took over the house band at Currie's Club Tropicana—Ben Branch and the Largos. They picked me up as their drummer. I couldn't have been happier, working at my home club where I took early inspiration. This place educated me. These men educated me. My friend Floyd Newman played baritone. He made some of the first hits at Satellite and Stax Records. Largos guitarist Clarence Nelson had so many ideas. He'd choke the guitar. Didn't play notes. Played rhythm. Played the shuffle like I did on drums. He choked the string and strummed chunky. I still thrive on guitar rhythms, like I did throughout my years as a recording artist, working with Steve Cropper and Teenie Hodges.

The Largos played the hit records to get everybody moving on the dance floor. That shit would be cooking. Five Royales style, Midnighters style. They had me up there man, smokin'. The people danced off time, like they were skating, but it looked good.

The key for me was to play the shuffle. A shuffle is like a horse galloping. You gallop while the bass is walking. "Honky Tonk" by Bill Doggett was the first example of a shuffle I heard. The song had a funky blues guitar and that shuffle beat. Those were some of the key ingredients here. Think about the instrumentals coming out of Memphis from the Mar-Keys, Willie Mitchell, Gene "Bowlegs" Miller, they all had those similar ingredients. The guitarist and tenor player with Bill Doggett dominated the sound like Andrew Love and Wayne Jackson did with the Memphis Horns on Stax.

Through watching drummers like Bill Tyus, I picked up the ability to shuffle. B.B. King's tenor player told me, "I ain't heard nobody shuffle like you, you got a left hand and a right foot. Got a snap to it. When you're playing behind someone, try to push them off stage."

He was right. I was in a rush playing with Ben Branch, everything up-tempo, all night long. That's where I was. I didn't know anything about laid back. The way Ben Branch played, the tempo fit and it felt good—high energy. We were playing that music coming out of New Orleans—"Ooh Pooh Pah Doo." I learned those different rhythms from what DJs Moohah and Honeyboy were playing on WDIA.

Ben Branch and "Bowlegs" Miller, who I worked with later, organized their bands in the same way. They wrote charts, but they would give me the records and say, "Listen at the way they do it. You can't play exactly like it, but use what you hear out of it. Play like you—but come close."

They played just like the records from how the chart was written, and they accepted me for learning quick. The tempo had to be danceable. I got a feeling going through my bones. Made me happy. I listened to all kinds of records, I just went for rhythm. I knew how to transport the rhythms and play them my way. I had my own signature then, but didn't know it.

Before I got involved in the scene, this man used to come through my neighborhood in a white truck, working for Southern Music. He'd bring 45s, that's when they had jukeboxes in cafés. I saw him with records in his hand and he went in a café. I was standing across the street on the corner. I heard this music come out. I heard this fantastic rhythm. I said, "Wow." The rhythm picked me right up. I said, "I'd like to play that song."

That's how I got hip to what was going on. I would see that white truck stop at the café and know there's new music. I'd sit out and listen to the new songs. That was my future calling me. I later ended up working the best years of my life for the company that owned Southern.

Working with Ben Branch made me a better drummer. The experience of playing the hits got me ready to record. In fact, that experience became instrumental in making the first hit record of the Memphis sound.

The Memphis sound is all about that backbeat, all about that stomp. I built that sound working in clubs, and perfected the sound in the studio. My first opportunity to record came from my work in nightclubs.

Rufus Thomas would come in the clubs and listen at me playing. He knew everyone and he'd wave at me and tell me, "You're gonna be alright." I didn't know he was checking me out then. Piano player Bob Talley told him about me. They all knew I had my own style. Rufus came to me and said, "We gon' make a record. I want to see what we can do with you in the studio."

I had never been in a studio. Didn't know anything about it. But when I stepped foot in Satellite for the first time, I saw Floyd Newman and Gilbert Caple, standing there discussing something over a piece of paper on a music stand. I knew Floyd, but hadn't met Gilbert. Rufus's son Marvell sat down at the piano. Chips Moman, the recording engineer, came down from the booth to get me organized on the kit. First time I met Chips. I was looking the studio over, trying to see what it was like. I was excited. Rufus took the floor and started giving instructions on how he wanted the song. I didn't know how to put a song together, but Rufus did it off the top of his head. He hummed out what he heard—no written music, no charts. That's what we call head tunes. Come right out your head. As he told Wilbur Steinberg the bass line, he turned to me and said, "You stay right there, hold that time."

But the way Rufus arranged it at first didn't work. At Currie's we played Jesse Hill's "Ooh Poo Pah Do." Wilbur suggested that we try that rhythm with Rufus's song. Chips was listening in the control room. I played that rhythm and it was right on. Chips said, "That's it right there, that'll work!"

That put me in the pocket. I felt comfortable, like I was at home. Rufus sang the melody. I twisted the rhythm to suit him. They came together and Chips came out on the floor smiling, giving thumbs up, saying, "Let's cut it!"

Booker T. Jones was there playing baritone sax on the opening and in the breaks. I improvised the break beat. Rufus had his daughter Carla singing with him. The song was called, "'Cause I Love You," and it hit. That song happened like magic.

Rufus had his band, the Bear Cats, who played local gigs. He come to my mother's house one day, before he went on the air at WDIA at night. We were having a lawn party, and he got a couple of hot dogs and a co-cola. We were standing around the card tables in the backyard. Rufus wanted me to join the Bear Cats. My mother told Rufus, "You can take him, but you're responsible for him. Make sure nothin' happen to him." Rufus said, "I'll take care of him."

When he got on the radio that night he said, "Out at Miss Grimes's house, they havin' a bang dang good 'un. That's where the drummer lives."

Rufus and the Bear Cats played at the Chatterbox in West Memphis on Broadway. He never took me on anything big. We used to play up there in little cafés in Orange Mound. When I started playing with Rufus, he had a '59 four-door Chevrolet. That car fit every member of the band and held every instrument in the trunk. Luther Steinberg would put the bass fiddle down the middle; the top of it would be at the windshield, and the butt end at the back window. We had Ma Rainey with us. She sang old blues. Mickey Gregory, another Manassas cat who later played with Isaac Hayes, was our trumpeter. Never took Carla out there, but Rufus's son Marvell was with us. I heard from another musician that Marvell thought I played too slow. That kind of bothered me a little bit but I never paid it much mind.

Rufus mostly was an old blues singer and a make-up artist—he made up songs. All Rufus wanted was the shuffle. He'd say "gimme a shuffle, b-flat!" That's an easy, good sounding key. He made up his lyrics. I listened to him go, ridin' off the bass line, ridin' off the shuffle. I'm picking up on what he's doing. He went to singing Lee Dorsey stuff, "Sittin' on my la la waitin' for my ya ya," and that rhythm went another way. Rufus had rhythm in his mouth. That's what was happenin' and I got good at pickin' up set tones coming out the voice.

After we took everybody home, he would say, "I wanna see what's going on up at Sunbeam Mitchell's." The first time he took me up there, I saw this big band—Allen Jones playing bass, Charles "Guitar" Friday, Evelyn Young on alto, trumpeter Calvin Grimes. The bandleader whose name was Struction, the vocalist was James Austin. Those days they danced till the wee hours. The guys played at other clubs then came in for a jam session.

Rufus played Yazoo City, Mississippi. I didn't know where we were going. When we crossed the Tallahatchie Bridge, he said that's where they threw Emmett Till's body. I had bought *Jet* magazine and seen him all swollen up. That messed me all up. I didn't understand why we couldn't be among each other.

I was still in school when that first record came out and I hit them joints with Rufus. My family knew I had something and they didn't want any interruption. Mr. Able kept me on track. He said, "You can be great but you gotta work hard at it. It's okay to see your buddies for a minute. You can go down to the corner, just don't stay there."

Well, that seemed like good advice, but I had no instrument. On gigs I'd always used the house drum kit. At home I'd spend hours tapping my drumsticks along with the radio. WDIA and WLOK kept my education going all day and night. My brother brought home some ice cream barrels from the Victory Sundry. They were empty, shaped just like drums. I set them up like a kit and had an old rack fan for a cymbal. I got something out of that stuff. My grandaddy's room was silent, with an old hollow floor. I stayed with those records and made no mistakes.

In the band room at Manassas, Mr. Able put charts in front of me, so I got some experience working off sheet music. The drum lines look like a spoon, with beats on the 1,2 and a rest, or the 1,2,3 and rest.

I worked at Currie's with the Largos on Monday night, Friday and Saturday. My friend Flop used to clean up the club to get it ready for the night. Mr. Currie had an old piano sitting in the corner. When Isaac Hayes got out of school, he'd sit at that piano. Flop let him in. Flop told me, "Isaac sits up here and plays this piano from the time he gets out of school until y'all come to work." That old piano was out of tune and missing half the keys, but Isaac would sit there and play on it.

We used to play for social clubs who'd meet at Currie's. Toppers Ball was one of the best. Mister Howard Bradshaw was with the Toppers, and he was always for me. He liked Isaac, too. The Toppers had their gathering at Currie's one night and they wanted to hear Isaac sing. Ben Branch was leading the band, and he didn't like Isaac for some reason. Ben Branch wouldn't let Isaac sing. Isaac was just there to check us out, he wasn't with the band. I don't know why Ben Branch objected to Isaac, but Isaac didn't have anything but the clothes on his back and the shoes on his feet. He didn't look presentable, clean like the band was dressed. He looked poor, though he had a big heart. He kept pushing ahead to his dreams, even though people like Ben Branch didn't get it.

Like with the home economics teacher, fate sometimes had this way of stepping in for Isaac. That night of the Toppers Ball, Mr. Bradshaw went over Ben's head to Mr. Currie. Ben Branch didn't care for that, and he could be quick-tempered, but Mr. Currie said to let Isaac sing or he'd be out of a job. So, Isaac wanted to sing "Just a Matter of Time," like he'd done at the school talent show. We were getting ready to play the Starlite Revue behind Brook Benton, so we knew the song. We had learned that for the big show that weekend with WDIA. Isaac come up there and the whole house went up. He got me, man. I had been playing with him at school but didn't know he could be so powerful. The next day, that's all you could hear up and down Thomas Street—"Man, Isaac Hayes killed it last night, y'all missed it. He goin' places." I knew then.

On top of what Isaac did with Mr. Able, there's another funny story about how he got his revenge after he'd made it. I left the Largos to join Gene "Bowlegs" Miller's group. Bowlegs hired Isaac and we were playing at a big club in Memphis called the Rosewood. Isaac and his partner Gilmore, tenor player, used to run around a neighborhood called Scutterfield. They had a group called the Magicians, with Sidney Kirk, keyboard player.

Sidney Kirk was always a jazz pianist and Gilmore knew jazz, too. Isaac still wasn't very good yet but from the things he learned, his skills started developing.

I never will forget, Isaac and Bowlegs got to arguing. Hank Crawford—another great from Manassas High School, he had left town to lead the Ray Charles band—had come in the door to listen at Bowlegs. I was standing talking to Hank while Bowlegs and Isaac argued.

Bowlegs said to Isaac, "Boy, you'll never go anywhere." Isaac told him, "Motherfucker, I'll show you. I'm better than you. I'm gonna have you working with me one day, watch what I tell you."

Bowlegs said, "That'll never happen, and you'll be back, on your knees."

Isaac said, "I doubt that. I'm a show you better than that."

When it did happen, Isaac had Bowlegs working for him, Mr. Able working for him— it's amazing the way all that revolved.

I had a helping hand in Isaac's breakthrough. He asked me to take him to Stax while I was doing session work. He said, "If I can just get a foot in the door, I'll show 'em what I got." I brought him there, I believe, for the first time.

CHAPTER FIVE

After Rufus and Carla Thomas hit with "'Cause I Love You" in 1960, things started happening with Satellite Records. Two more songs made money—"Gee Whiz" by Carla Thomas, and "You Don't Miss Your Water," by William Bell. I played drums on both tracks.

We didn't cut "Gee Whiz" at the Satellite/Stax studio. A machine broke and we had to scramble to find another studio. We ended up about a mile down the road from Stax at Royal Recording. That's the first time I set foot in that place, and the first time I met Willie Mitchell.

"Gee Whiz" is special for having two great producers and recording engineers involved, Chips Moman and Willie Mitchell. I could tell by the conversation those two had, they both lived and breathed music. Willie got Chips up to speed on the board, and Willie mostly observed while Chips ran the session. Willie was so cool and laid back.

That's also the first time I saw Noel Gilbert and his family from the Memphis Symphony Orchestra string section. Being around musicians of that caliber elevated me. I think I played "Gee Whiz" with brushes. We worked hard and that was a more complicated arrangement, with the strings, but it all paid off with a great record. It's funny, everyone knows and remembers the records, but those sessions took just a day. Playing shows was almost our whole life.

My first opportunity to play behind established stars came with the WDIA Goodwill Revue and the Starlight Revue. They had two big shows a year. WDIA cut deals, put the packages together to bring in artists, and in exchange gave them airplay and a hotel room.

Onzie Horne, the old band director at my school, Manassas High, who played with B.B. King, directed the WDIA revue band. Bowlegs Miller handled the arrangements. These were package shows of all the top hit artists. They'd come out for one or two songs, but we stayed on all night. We had to learn every hit. We rehearsed for a few days before the show, which was always held on a Saturday night. Those shows took place downtown at Ellis Auditorium.

The show started at eight with gospel—Swan Silvertones, Highway QCs, Golden Gate Quartet, Spirit of Memphis, Dixie Hummingbirds. I didn't play behind any of them; they were quartets, with their own guitar or piano, plus hand-clapping and foot stomping. The harmony was so tight and beautiful, they grooved. You could feel it.

The band set up in what's called the snake pit, but the drums were elevated so that everybody could see me. Mr. Horne would be out there conducting, with the light on his sheet music.

I backed Jo Jo Benson, Bo Diddley, Dee Clark, Jackie Wilson. As a kid, my friends and I listened to Mickey and Sylvia and Fats Domino. I ended up playing with all of them. They put their foot down and said how it had to be. You had to have your thinking cap on. Marvin Gaye came to play the revue before he was a star, and I backed him live on "Hitch Hike."

I kept busy in the clubs with the future stars as well. After Isaac left Bowlegs, we went over to the Plantation Inn, West Memphis, playing in a combo with Floyd Newman on horn and Joe Woods on guitar. The group recorded "Frog Stomp" for Stax, a great instrumental. When we played that song live, Floyd said, "That's you, man. That beat is your identity. No other drummer can play that." We went to the studio because of that beat. Isaac is on top with the organ, I'm driving the rhythm with the foot, playing 4-4 on the bass drum, and 6-8 on the high-hat.

We came up with the B-side, "Sassy" by me humming the melody and Isaac picking up on that. It wasn't nothing but Bill Doggett-style, instrumental music. I saw Joe Woods look up at Floyd. I heard Floyd blowing it, softly. Like he's breathing. I never said anything about it, but I wrote that song, and they jumped on it. I never received credit. I left it alone. It took me a long time to understand business; my head stayed in music.

Floyd always looked out for me on the road. When I went on my first tour, he told me how important it was to leave women alone. He said when he played in B.B. King's band, one of the musicians in the group talked to a woman in the audience and her husband came right up and blew the musician away. That scared me.

At the Plantation, we played blues and rock 'n' roll behind a singer known as Sissy Charles. Strange cat. He looked like a gorilla. You could see the sassiness in him by the way he walked and how he looked at you. Floyd and him got along, but he'd look at me and throw his nose up. He was one of the best blues singers we had. That Sissy Charles was a trip. I ain't had too much to do with him. I was scared of that motherfucker. Strong as an ox. Hair stood out here like a caveman. White people loved him; he played at white clubs. He worked at the Plantation and then he'd go sing all night for fun at Sunbeam's. Sissy Charles—nobody gave a fuck about him being gay.

All kinds of colorful characters stuck around the music scene. Like Sissy Charles, there was a guy called Peaches who dressed like a woman. It ain't nothing new. Peaches was funky, but everyone from Manassas High knew Peaches, and my mentor Mr. Able said Peaches was very talented coming up. These were just regular people in our lives. Peaches led a marching band of kids through the neighborhood. They had their little uniforms. There was a whole lot of pride. Don't come at Peaches wrong at the Sissy Ball up at the Flamingo Room or you're liable to get cut. But Peaches was about community.

Another great, Ms. Shake Right, could dance the life back into a dead man. She had a trick where she screwed a light bulb into her vagina and that sucker would turn on. I played drums behind her while she did this and always wondered about the trick. I thought she must have something hot in there. But, Ms. Shake Right was my friend's mother. Wasn't anything nasty about her, she's a good person who knew how to perform and did her thing to take care of her family. Ms. Shake Right was a lovely woman.

Working with Sissy Charles, I learned certain things from playing white clubs. White people danced off beat, they were all in different time and doing different moves. The first time I saw it, I laughed to myself. They were on the beat as long as they could hear it, but got lost off the beat. In white clubs, I never saw fighting, hatred, or negativity. That gave me a different view of white people from other African Americans. I still don't like to hear black people disparage whites.

Black clubs stayed pretty wild. When the Largos played "Slummer the Slum" in Currie's, the people would break out into fights. Mr. Currie told us, "Don't y'all sing that song cause they tear up my tables and chairs." I don't know why that song would make people fight, but certain songs you'd play got people riled up.

Down there on Beale Street, the Flamingo was that way, Club Handy too. I didn't like to be caught up in there because I didn't know what song was going to start a fight or if they'd already played that one. I kept my eyes on the door in a club.

Mr. Currie had seven or eight bouncers in his club. Sunbeam had about the same. And his pistol. Sunbeam had a tough little guy called Willie Britt working the floor with his little baseball bat. He'd whoop your ass with that thing. They'd get through and throw you down them long steps down to the street. Sunbeam's piano player Struction would get into the fights, too. I never knew why he'd want to do that, I'd want to just stay out of it if I was on stage. But Struction was bandleader, so I guess he wanted to take charge.

My mama came to see me play once at Currie's. She'd stopped going out as much as she used to. She said she didn't want to bother me by being there but everybody kept telling her how well I was doing, so she came to see for herself. That was the only time she saw me play. She got happy that night and made me feel good.

Mama loved my music. She'd play my songs on the jukebox in the café. I'd stop in and see her there. She'd kiss me on the jaw and say, "You want a glass of cold beer?" I'd drink one with her and her friends and she'd say, "That's my son, playing them drums."

I stayed with Ben Branch and the Largos until he left to work with Operation Breadbasket in Chicago for Dr. Martin Luther King. A lot of people know about Ben Branch from that part of his life. He was the last person Dr. King spoke to before dying. Ben had trouble with drummers up in Chicago. He sent me a letter and wanted me to come up because he was used to Memphis drummers. I couldn't go, because Lorice Thompson had reformed the Largos. I had been with him and wanted to stay on.

That's where the album *Beale Street Today* came from. Dot Records put it out in 1963. The session wasn't overly professional. We didn't have a bass player. Clarence Nelson didn't show up, so we just had to use what we had. My schoolmate William Allen played organ and he played the bass line, like you hear in church. There was Harvey Simmons on tenor, Calvin Grimes on trumpet, Pee Wee, George, Willie, Roosevelt, Lorice, and that was it. We played our regular covers on that record and said we were playing in a Beale Street club even though we were at Currie's in North Memphis. I stayed on with the Largos another two years and then went with Bowlegs.

I was still staying with my mother in New Chicago. When I was working at the Flamingo Room with Bowlegs, I used to catch the Chelsea 8 bus going downtown and it would put me off in front of the Malco Theater at Main and Beale. There was a fruit stand across the street where the old man had beautiful fruit laid out. He used to give me a orange, apple, pear, or something. I'd have my suit and my bag, going to work. I wore a dark suit, white shirt and tie. That's when musicians wore sharkskin suits, Stacy Adams shoes.

We dressed to look presentable. The club owners wanted us to look professional, like we belonged playing for a respectable audience. Ben Branch and Bowlegs gave their musicians coats. One had designs like money on it. We looked clean. Most of the audience dressed up, too. We couldn't do like you see the guys do today.

As I walked down Beale to my gig, Sunbeam's band would already be playing up at Club Handy, and I could hear them when I get to the corner of Beale and Second outside Lansky Brothers. That's where all the entertainers got their suits. Sunbeam had the big band and they'd be dressed like Lawrence Welk's group—sharp. They wore gold, plaid, or blue, with bow ties. In the summertime at night, all the windows would be open. People didn't have anything but fans to keep them cool. So I could hear that band coming all the way down Beale Street. That band would be shouting, they sounded so good.

The street smelled of popcorn, hot dogs. You'd see people eating those One Minute hot dogs, drinking beer. It was a place of joy.

When I got to Handy Park, corner of Beale and Hernando, I loop up to my gig at the Flamingo Room. Around the park you'd see harmonica players, banjo players, all kinds of talent would be out on that street. An itty-bitty woman played blues in the park during the daytime with the old blues harmonica players doing their thing. Something always happened on Beale Street. Music would always be the number one priority; it'd never be a quiet day.

For the Halloween Ball at the Flamingo, they'd go out and get scarecrows, pumpkins, women would come out and dress the club up. That started around ten o'clock. People came out in their costumes. I miss that, it was the best. That club would be packed. People had the time of their lives. After it was all over, they went up to the Harlem House to eat, maybe a hot dog special or Salisbury steak and hash browns, cherry Coke, apple or pecan pie, and it was on. Good eating.

Black police walked the street at that time. Tom Marshall walked the street, Ben Whitney walked the street. Shug Jones was mainly at Beale and Hernando around the theaters, the New Daisy, the Old Daisy, the Palace. Where most of the blacks accumulated, that was the spot, near Handy Park, Club Handy, the Flamingo. Then you had the Blue Stallion. The Harlem House restaurant was right next to the New Daisy, and then you had another Harlem House around on Hernando. Nice place. Culpepper's, across the street, stayed open until four in the morning, selling good hot barbecue. The Velvet Club was next door. Very nice place. Red and white furniture, very low light. But people gravitate to the big clubs so I didn't see too much happening there. Officer Shug Jones, that was his beat, and he controlled that block. If he told you something, that's what he meant. He tell you to move on, you'd better. A lot of people got their asses whooped down there. A lot of people got put in the Black Maria. It looked like a dog wagon. They put your ass in that and carry it to jail.

All the pimps drove around in their Cadillac cars. They had the flying lady hood ornament, and they spotlighted that flying lady. That's how you could tell it was a pimp. The police were kind of hooked in with it. Whatever arrangement had taken place down-town, pimping was allowed. Police knew what the girls were doing and what the pimps were doing. That did something for this city, as far as raking in money. I never was in it, and I never wanted to make an enemy. I only took in what they wanted to let me know.

There was a shoeshine stand outside Club Handy that could hold about four people at a time. I'd look in there and think the guy shining shoes was short, but come to find out, he had kneepads on and he'd stay down on the floor working. We'd take our suits to the cleaners around there, too. That little area around Handy Park was full of good times.

Back down towards Main at Beale and Second they had dry goods, tailor shops, and pawn shops. A couple of cafés down there would be clean. You could always ride through that intersection and hear music from jukeboxes—Chuck Willis, Little Willie John, Big

Joe Turner. I paid attention to all of the music I heard coming out of the jukeboxes. Same way I did at home in North Memphis on Bellevue.

The Flamingo was an upstairs room with old hardwood floors. It had a Western saloon bar with a little swinging door on the side, chairs, tables with tablecloths. The interior was wood-grained around the walls. The bandstand was so high, maybe six or seven feet up. It was built up where people could see from the back. The dance floor spread out wide, but the owner Clifford Miller might cover up the dance floor with chairs for a big act. Unlike a lot of those joints, the back of the house was even nice, laid out with dressing rooms. A fire escape led out the back, and a double staircase led up to the front.

The Flamingo would hardly ever be open unless they had something going on at night. I'd stop in during the daytime and see my friend Bilbo in there cleaning the place up, getting it ready for the night. I'd go through and take a peek, jive with him a minute.

Playing in the Flamingo with the Bowlegs Miller band, we opened up our show with a high-energy instrumental to get everyone stretched out and ready to play. Bowlegs would do a couple songs that he had recorded, and after that, Spencer Wiggins would come out to sing, and he'd go for thirty, thirty-five minutes. Marino Choice sang for maybe fifteen or twenty. Spencer was top notch, but Clifford liked to have two acts. Marino Choice was like Jackie Wilson, he did turns and splits. He was always on Beale Street, every day. You didn't see Spencer like that. Marino wore a handkerchief tied over his process in the daytime. He'd be in the joints, the pool hall, with the folks that hung out down there.

On stage, Bowlegs could crack jokes. He knew gimmicks and how to put shows on. He knew how to sell tickets to get people into a club. He was just professional, a master. He worked hard. I felt comfortable playing with him because he set the time. He used to tell me, "If ya can't feel the beat, the music ain't got any soul."

Bowlegs played top records from the radio. Our vocalist Spencer Wiggins sung the top songs. That's how they packed the club. You could tell when you hit the people with one of their favorite records and hear the women holler. You know something's going down. It always made me feel good, because we wanted to reach the people. The records played on the radio is the stuff we played in the clubs. Bowlegs and Ben Branch were both top notch. Funny with the money, but excellent musically.

It's interesting though, working in a recording studio had a completely different power structure. Bowlegs Miller was a star and bandleader in the clubs and then it flip-flopped in the recording studio. He'd do a session in the horn section for Willie Mitchell, and he and Willie fell out, arguing over the way one note should be played. Bowlegs wasn't the leader in Willie's studio, and if Willie wanted you to play a certain note in a certain place, that's what you did. Bowlegs would fuss, "That ain't the right note," and Willie would say, "Just play the motherfucker that's on the paper." I saw that happen. You put too many leaders together to try to get something done, that leads to problems. To see them work through it, forget about their trouble and treat each other like brothers inspired me as a man and musician.

One of the signatures of the Memphis sound came out of those clubs we played every night. The Flamingo Room and Sunbeam's Club Handy both had organs. A man named "Blind Oscar" played organ up at the Handy—he was bad. Between Booker T. Jones at Stax and Charles Hodges at Hi, that organ became part of the soul of the Memphis sound. Take those clubs out of the picture of Memphis music and there isn't any picture.

CHAPTER SIX

The fame of our first hits, "'Cause I Love You" and "Gee Whiz," caused the company that started out as Satellite Records to change its name. From then on it was Stax Records. The owners were Jim Stewart—he put the ST in Stax—and Estelle Axton. She put the AX in Stax.

The first hit on Stax Records was William Bell's, "You Don't Miss Your Water." Of all the stars from those days, he's going strongest now. William is a professional and always has been. Very clean cut and business-like.

When I went into the studio for that session, I noticed this cymbal that sat in the corner. Chips Moman, the recording engineer and producer of those early Stax hits, told me it's a rivet cymbal. I walked by and tapped the stick on it and it made a new sound to me. I said I'm gonna play this sucker. Chips gave me the smile and the thumbs up. That made me feel good. That cymbal changed the rhythm and Chips enhanced it. That cymbal coats the sound. That helped make the record "You Don't Miss Your Water."

At Satellite/Stax, it was still almost all white when I got down there, except Gilbert Caple, Floyd Newman, and Booker T. The racial feeling at the studio took time to warm up. The house band at Stax during the early sixties was a white band, the Mar-Keys. They had a hit called "Last Night," and went on tour. Well, they didn't send Floyd Newman with the group. He was a black horn player who sang the line, "Oooooh, last night."

The drummer on the recording, a black musician named Curtis Green, didn't go either. He could play on the level of anybody in Memphis. Curtis fussed about money and the club owners and bandleaders all acted funny about money. Curtis got in an argument with Sunbeam Mitchell. A bass player from Sunbeam's named Frog told me what happened. He said, "Sunbeam wouldn't give Curtis his money. Curtis picked up a chair and hit Sunbeam across the head and ran out the club." Well, Sunbeam would shoot someone for less. Curtis had to leave town and we didn't hear from him for a long time. So, that was a decent excuse for why he didn't travel with the Mar-Keys.

Still, they didn't send the black musicians out on tour, only the whites went to do shows to support the record. I heard a rumor that the all-white Mar-Keys flopped out on the road, and that helped lead the change to more black musicians getting work at Satellite studio. I heard that the Mar-Keys went to Detroit, and the club owner sent them away and said to bring him the band that played on the record. People in the studio talked about things like that.

When they found out the Mar-Keys drummer couldn't hold time, Chips Moman recommended me to do more sessions. Once Chips got me, I went to growing. I cut everything for the Mar-Keys after "Last Night," but I never felt accepted as a member. No matter what, I am a Mar-Key.

In those early days at Satellite we couldn't be seen coming out of the building together, even though we'd played together in the studio. We'd pool our money together to buy bread and bologna, soft drinks—wasn't any beer drinking—and we all ate together. I miss it. We had to be careful outside because we didn't want any trouble for the studio.

Because of growing up in music, I have a different view on race from most other African Americans in Memphis. Working at the Rivermont, the Hi-Hat, and the Plantation Inn, I saw prosperous whites. They always treated me nicely. The activity in clubs stayed calm and happy. I appreciated what they paid me. I knew that bad things were happening out there, but I saw kindness and I had hope that the city could get along beautifully. In clubs, black audiences turn their nose up at their own. I saw the love from Caucasian audiences. They were all about fun and they paid far better than black clubs. I saw joy there. I never saw a white person troubled. No fights.

People at Stax tended their business. Chips played music and always fooled around on the guitar or blew his harmonica when we weren't cutting. Miss Axton stayed in the shop up front. Mr. Stewart worked in his office; we didn't see too much of him. Nobody around there drank or sweet-talked anybody. The place seemed clean-cut. People worked like a regular job.

I showed up, did my sessions, and got off the clock. I never have been one to hang around. I earned a session fee but didn't understand the business. I helped them grow but never had that perspective. I was just there to cut. They had a whole gang of musicians coming through at that time, looking for a hit.

I cut Prince Conley, a local blues singer who wore gaucho clothes. He sang "I'm Going Home." I remember Steve Cropper being on that session. Prince Conley worked in Sunbeam Mitchell's band at Club Handy.

By the time I started regularly recording at Stax, Booker T. Jones had already become a fixture around the studio. Booker never said much. He stayed on the keyboards. That's where his head was. Booker was deep, all the time. I sat across from him in the drum booth and watched him on the organ. I locked into him when we played.

Booker T. used to sit at the piano and mess around. I listened to him and started playing on his rhythm. Booker looked at me and nodded. Floyd Newman and the horns fell in. That's how we cut my favorite Mar-Keys record, "Sailor Man Waltz." The song is based on Ray Charles' "Blues Waltz."

Jim Stewart bought a brand new Hammond B-3 organ, and Booker T. was just messing around with it, and came up with

"Pop-Eye Stroll." He's just trying to learn, pulling the stops, and he found the sound. Booker played a lot of what I call circus music. I was sitting there laughing at him. Marvell was sitting there laughing. But Chips said, "I like that. Let's cut it." We got serious. Steve played a line on the guitar, Marvell started playing, and this thing came together. Before we knew it, we had a song.

The rhythm is a little more in the pocket than the up-tempo stuff I was used to, and a little more like what I think I'm known for now. The song shows how creative Booker could be on the fly. He's a genius. I admire him. I learned from him. He had all kinds of things running in his head. I always wondered what he would play next.

We created on the go. It was all head tunes, and we'd blend ideas. Somebody played a line, somebody'd take the line, and we go from there. Chips more or less got everything sounding right and stayed out of the way. We never thought about who wrote the song and would get credit. We felt happy to cut records and have fun.

The song "Burnt Biscuits," released by the Triumphs, though it's basically the same group as on the Mar-Keys records, came from the Five Royales' "Slummer the Slum"—that's the song that used to start fights at Currie's. I brought that beat to the song, but I knew I couldn't play it the same way. I did what I call turning the beat around. That's how you make money off of an idea, you take it and turn it around, so it's not the same as what's out. You rearrange the beat that's known so that when people hear you it's fresh sounding but familiar.

I cut with Sam Jones and the Veltones. They were called the Canes for their session. They were managed by a disc jockey from local radio station WLOK named Dick "Cane" Cole, a good friend of Sunbeam Mitchell who ran Club Handy. The Canes' "Why Should I Suffer With the Blues" sounds like the music I heard at Club Handy—heavy Ray Charles influence.

Working with Booker had gone well, but I had got out of pocket on the day they ended up cutting "Green Onions." I still enjoyed playing ball and had been down in the park when they called me. When I got home that evening my mama told me I'd missed a phone call.

That could have been my shot. Steve Cropper recommended using Al Jackson Jr. who played drums at that time with Willie Mitchell at the Manhattan Club. My mentor Mr. Able used to say that Al taking over for me at Stax was a pussy deal. Al and his lady were swinging with some of the folks over there. He started getting called in for sessions over me. That's when they cut "Green Onions." The rest is history.

With Al Jackson, it's almost like he was following me, or I was following him. I joined Bowlegs when Al left to play in Willie Mitchell's band, and then I took Al's spot in Willie's band once Al left. Then he came to record at Stax and Hi after I had started in both.

Al played more quick and light than I do. He played a twenty-two-inch ride cymbal, a great cymbal. You hear it on so much Stax stuff. His set had a sixteen-inch floor tom, fourteen-inch tom-tom, fourteen-inch snare, fourteen-inch high-hats, and fifteen-inch crash.

Some fans want to compare us and some even want to put us against each other. Me and Al were great friends. We had no rivalry at all except a friendly one. Willie Mitchell worked with both of us, and probably knew us better than anyone else did, so he's the best to make comparisons. Willie said, "What better drummers could I have than Al Jackson and Howard Grimes? The best of two worlds." I had never really thought about how connected Al and I were until I heard Willie say that. Willie said Al had the talent to tear a song completely down and build it back a different way. Willie said I had more creativity and ideas with rhythm.

I only knew of Al when "Green Onions" came out; we hadn't met. Musicians called him "Little Al" because his father used to lead a band, and all the music people in Memphis knew Al Jackson Sr. When I heard "Green Onions" I thought the drumming wasn't anything I couldn't do. He put the foot on the 2-4, following the bass.

Al excited me the first time I saw him perform, with Bowlegs. In fact Al had cut with Bowlegs an instrumental called "One More Time," for Vee-Jay. The sound echoes what Satellite had begun with "Last Night." After "One More Time," Bowlegs left Memphis for Minnesota. When he came back, they had a celebration at Currie's. That's when I first saw Al Jackson.

Before Al left the Willie Mitchell band, I traveled with Booker, Duck, and those guys, when "Green Onions" was hot, so I've played that song live.

Once in Detroit, Duck and some of them went and bought some pussy. They came and got me and Booker and brought us to this old room with a woodstove and a sheet hung up. A lady came from behind that sheet, and Booker said, "Man, we need to go on back to our room. I don't want none of this." I said, "Me and you both."

I still did some Stax sessions after Al got in. I played on the Wendy Rene song, "Bar-B-Que," and did Barbara and the Browns' 1964 hit "Big Party." The great Clarence Nelson, my man from the Largos, played guitar on that. Clarence and the whole group were whiskey heads. He had a great style, based on Lowman Pauling from the Five Royales, who spent time in Memphis playing at Currie's and recording for Willie Mitchell at Home of the Blues records on Beale Street.

Steve Cropper studied Pauling too. I worked some with Cropper. Steve hung around Jim Stewart a lot, looked to me like they collaborated. Steve wrote the beat for Eddie Floyd's song "On a Saturday Night." It took me a while to get that beat, but once I got it—hit record. I took that beat over to Hi, used it on Denise LaSalle's first hit, "Trapped By A Thing Called Love." I still use old beats on certain sessions today. It has to be the right song.

The most complicated rhythm I ever cut ended up on an Ivory Joe Hunter B-side that I cut at Stax in the early sixties, "That Kind of Woman." I played a bongo with the sticks while working the kit. I used the bongo instead of cymbals. Duck had a deep bass line on that. I couldn't hear anything else. He'd get his head bobbing and just was feeling it. Steve and him felt each other. Him and Steve got in their groove. Steve's clean on the guitar—no static, no feedback. I never heard Steve's hand move on the strings he played so clean. We cut some unbelievable B-sides. We never knew where a record would be placed, so we gave it everything, every time.

Working around there, I came to love Miss Estelle Axton. She co-owned the Stax label and studio with her brother, Jim Stewart. Miss Axton just glowed. She'd give me ideas. She asked me to make a funky beat with a marching band cadence. I mixed a Five Royales rhythm with the Ray Charles beat on "Mary Ann." I played like I did in the Paradise Park drum and bugle corps and we came up with "Yank Me Doodle." We did that as the Barracudas. That came from Miss Axton—she wanted to put the whistles and the 1776 sound to something funky. We don't have people like Miss Axton to motivate musicians and writers. Rufus Thomas played that record on WDIA and broke it.

The only song I ever cut that I hate is by Sam and Dave, the one Teenie Hodges wrote, called, "I Take What I Want." The spirit is wrong.

When I took Isaac Hayes to Stax, he hooked up with David Porter. They wrote Sam and Dave's first hit, "Good Night Baby." I played on it, and that's the closest me and Isaac got to working together in the studio.

Out of Sam and Dave, I like Dave. Me and Dave were cool. Sam doesn't have too much to say to me nowadays. Recently we were both up at the Stax Museum. He told his wife, "This man cut my first hit record." I said, "I didn't know you knew that." He always thought he was big shit. Dave and me were real buddies. Dave said, "Goddamn, Howard Grimes the playin'est motherfucker I ever heard in my life. He put that shit down, boy." Sam never had much to say. God rest the soul of Dave.

CHAPTER SEVEN

Seeing things around my neighborhood growing up, I learned to be careful around women. Often, I saw this nice gentleman known as Odie B. Quiet cat, like me. Clean cut. He knew my mama. He had an eggshell white and blue '55 Pontiac. Odie B. got off from work one day at Firestone. I was standing on the corner. I saw him stop in to drink a beer at the café next to my uncle's.

This woman at the café always created problems, fucking with men. She told her boyfriend Odie B. had tried to kiss her. Odie B's sitting in there by himself having a beer. The guy didn't ask him anything, just took the woman's word. He hit Odie B. in the mouth and busted his lip. Blood ran down the side of his mouth. Odie B. didn't say one word. He walked out the door, walked to his car across the street, opened up the trunk of his car. He had that '55 parked outside Chappy's Barber Shop. He got his pistol out. Odie B. went back into the café and blew that cat away.

Odie B. sat right there until the police came. Cat was laying there dead on the floor. She was sitting up there weeping, "He killed my man." Everyone knew she'd started the problem. She got him killed, over nothing. The police told Odie B. to go home. They barred him from New Chicago. Never took him to jail.

That's the reason I don't jump to conclusions based on what somebody says. I saw that happen with Odie B. Unlucky for me, that still wasn't enough to keep my life free from that kind of trouble.

My first wife brought me nothing but pain. My mother didn't come to the wedding. My granddaddy told me, "Son, if you've got to fight a woman, you don't need her." But my nose was open. She popped pills and drank and lived faster than me. She courted other men while I worked. I was just so much in love with her. That's what started me drinking. I thought if I did it with her, it would be all right, but that just made everything worse. I wasn't hooked on alcohol, but I only did it to prove something to my wife. Meanwhile, she was steady running games on me.

I wanted a real family and to be with the woman I loved. I could accept difficulty, and believed that things would turn around if I could be patient. I believed in standing beside my woman. I know now that I trusted her too much, and how naïve I was.

I had moved in with her family. Her mama said since we were living together, we should marry. I thought that was right and fair. My wife-to-be kept pressing me. This is where my trouble started. We were married in March of 1966. The day we got married, I had no money. We got married by a pimp her mama was going with. He hauled pasteboard boxes for a living. I always said he's the devil, dark as he is. On Thursday evenings, he'd pick up my wife's mother. They'd go, get a room, come back at twelve or one. She'd get out of the car, and he'd go on back to his wife. I didn't like it.

I took my wife to the New Daisy the night we got married. She started acting crazy. We went home, and I thought we were going to get intimate, but she went off. Her mama was in the next room, nitpicking, instigating. My wife snapped. Out came her pistol. She said, "I'm gonna kill you." She pulled the trigger three times— it didn't fire. I knocked the gun out of her hand. I slapped her. I jumped out the door and went to get a room at the Holiday Inn. I stayed there until things cooled off.

As hectic as my personal life had gotten, things kept happening for me in music. After recording Carla Thomas's "Gee Whiz" at Royal Studios, my next session there took place in 1966. Bowlegs

Miller brought me there to record Little Junior Parker for Mercury Records. I'd listened to Junior Parker on the jukebox—"Annie Get Your Yo Yo," and things like that. I never thought I'd record with him.

Junior Parker drank J&B Scotch. Cool as can be. I didn't know why he had to have that drink, but once he did, the song came out of him. We did one called "Just Like a Fish." I did a whole album on Junior Parker. He wasn't hard to get along with or arrogant.

As a drummer, I felt lucky among musicians. A lot of them said, "Don't mess with the drummer—he can make you look bad." A drummer can break up your timing and throw you off, and you can't get out of it. I never played that trick, but I think that power makes the singers treat us drummers a little better.

In 1967, my old producer at Stax, Chips Moman, recommended me to the leader of a group called Flash and the Board of Directors. That was a white group—Flash's real last name is Fleischman—all great guys. Flash and the Board of Directors played rock. We covered "Midnight Hour," "Born on the Bayou," "Nowhere Man." I wore my tall boots and Robin Hood hat on stage.

We started working at the Thunderbird. That place was popular, an integrated club. Everybody got along. They came for fun, drinking, music, and the women. The place was semi-underground, in the basement of a tower at Poplar Avenue and Manassas Street in Memphis. The Thunderbird was more of a young counterculture scene than anything else in Memphis.

After work at the club, I'd go over to the Harlem House restaurant in North Memphis to have breakfast. Late night people would be in having a hot dog and playing the jukebox. That's where I first heard Willie Mitchell's music. I liked the style, so I stood up, went to see who's song was playing, and that's how I learned his name. After that, I'd always put a Willie Mitchell record on the box.

I played pretty well with the different combos and big bands, Floyd Newman, Bowlegs, Ben Branch, and Flash. Now I wondered if I could hang with Willie Mitchell. Meanwhile, I didn't know it, but Willie had come to check me out.

Teenie Hodges came to see me play with Flash at the Thunderbird. He came up, introduced himself as Willie Mitchell's guitarist, and said Al Jackson was getting ready to leave Willie's band. He said he thought I could play with them. "I know he'll like you," Teenie said. Excited as I was, at the moment, I couldn't do anything about it. I was getting ready to go on tour with Paul Revere and the Raiders. What happened out there made me want to stay off the road forever.

Flash and the Board of Directors had become the back-up band for big package tours in the South. The band backed up B.J. Thomas, Dusty Springfield. Any star who came to Memphis to record came down to the Thunderbird to sit in with Flash. That's how we hooked up with Paul Revere, thanks to Jerry Williams, a man who helped organize those tours.

I had never been out and wanted go. This was my chance. My top priority was to take care of my mother. That was my purpose. But I didn't realize what I was getting ready to face. Mark Lindsay, the lead singer of Paul Revere and the Raiders, told me he'd stay close. I wondered what he meant. I was the only black member of the group, and they knew things might get strange.

Mostly nobody cared. It was all business. Traveling on the bus was smooth. That thing had gotten outfitted with bunk beds. We rested well, but had no time to spare. We played huge crowds, over 50,000 people in stadiums, 15,000 in coliseums. I'd never seen anything close to it. We worked a lot of dates for Dick Clark. I was fascinated just to be out there. Paul Revere and the Raiders had massive hit records, thousands of kids screaming, like at the Beatles shows.

We were in Dallas when some hanger-on's fiancée or girlfriend said to the band, "I see you're a bunch of nigger lovers." They told her off and said for me to not let her kind worry me. Well, I didn't, but that let me know what it could be like. Still, nothing prepared me for how tough things got in Montgomery, Alabama. Almost everything had gone great until we got to Montgomery.

We'd been out a few weeks when the group had a gig at the Montgomery coliseum. Paul Revere and the Raiders were headlining. I didn't know it at the time, but Governor George Wallace's children were big Paul Revere and the Raiders fans. Dr. Martin Luther King Jr. had called Governor Wallace "the most dangerous racist in America." The group had played Montgomery before, and some of the guys had met the Wallace kids.

We got to the coliseum early to set up and do a sound check. I was getting the drums set up on an elevated platform. While I was busy with that the house manager went up to the tour manager, Jerry Williams, and asked, "What's that up there?"

Jerry asked me to come down to where they were talking. This house manager, Jerry, Flash, and our roadie Hoss, who's about 6'7" were there. I walked up. The house manager said, "The nigger ain't playin' in here. We never had James Brown in here. Ain't no nigger played in here. Ain't no nigger ever gonna play here. This my building."

Jerry spoke up. He said, "If Howard's not gonna play, then there's not gonna be a show. Furthermore, have you ever seen 12,000 kids tear a building down, brick by brick? I wish you a lot of luck." Jerry looked to Hoss and said, "Load it all back up, we're not playin'."

I went back to the bus. I really didn't want to go in that building again at that point. The guys were outside talking. The building manager kept saying the promoter had a contract and it was gonna be a $50,000 night.

Jerry went inside and got on the phone to call Paul Revere at the hotel. Paul was angry at what happened and agreed with calling off the show. Then Jerry called the state trooper who was his contact for Governor Wallace. The governor's children were supposed to come to the show. Well, before long he got on with Governor Wallace himself. By that time, Paul Revere had come to the coliseum.

Paul got on the bus with me.

Well, we didn't know it, but the wheels were turning. The state highway patrol started showing up. Seeing all those cops gathering around our bus, I was afraid. But Jerry let me know that the governor had gotten involved and said he wouldn't allow anything to happen to us. He said he'd call in the National Guard to protect us. They turned completely around. I didn't know what would go down inside the building, but I agreed to go ahead in and play.

They had the drums on a riser with an American flag. I was afraid to go up. They went and installed a second riser, so I was up above everybody on the stage. Their heads were level with the bottom of the drums. Our crew handled the lights for our show. The second we started, it had been arranged for every light in the building to shine on me. When we hit the first note, I was blinded. I was the only person on stage in light. My heart stopped for a second, until I took a breath.

Just then, the kids went crazy. It was such a warm feeling. They screamed like they had seen Elvis Presley. At intermission, the governor's children came backstage to visit and asked for my autograph. I signed their programs for them.

The next night in Miami, Mark Lindsay told me, "You did it, man, you broke world history." I don't look at it like that. I appreciate the way the band had stood with me more than anything else.

I have to thank Jerry Williams, not only for helping me through that situation and standing by me, but for doing an interview for this book and telling that story the way he lived it. Jerry was in the middle of that situation the whole time.

Back when I sat on the bus alone before Paul got on with me, before we went ahead with the show, I thought about how Teenie had come to me. It felt like I had gone on the road at the wrong time. I wanted that shot with Willie Mitchell's group.

CHAPTER EIGHT

One of the signatures of my style is the laid back feeling. I didn't always play this way. I got so relaxed from playing with Willie Mitchell. When I first met Willie, I was in a rush with my rhythm. The way Ben Branch, Bowlegs, and the young rockers played, the hot tempo fit and it felt good—high energy. When a drummer can groove, everybody takes that ride. It's love. It's happiness. People around me told me I was groovin'. They were always happy.

The day I went to audition at Hi, the band was there, and Willie gave me a tryout with them. I saw three brothers, Teenie, Charles, and Leroy Hodges. We got along great the moment I met them. They had nothing but fun and so much love between them. They talked about their family, all the wonderful people in their lives.

Willie said he'd gone through five drummers after Al Jackson left. I showed up with those Bowlegs and Ben Branch rhythms in my mind and just about followed the other five out the door. As my audition began, Willie set the time, and I started running with it. He stopped everything and said, "Hold it, the fuck you think you're doing?"

I said, "I'm trying to make your band."

I didn't know what else to say or do. He said, "Sloooow down, Goddammit! We gon' aaaaalllll get there at the saaaaaame time."

Willie had his own pace. I picked up the tone in his voice. Peace was there. He said, "Here's where I want it at. I want the motherfucker right there, so play it there."

The big test was Willie's hit "20-75," so that's what we played.

Bowlegs and Ben Branch had always said to play just like the record. That was my standard. I'd played the song on the Harlem House jukebox, and knew the beat. None of the other drummers he tried to use could play that song.

He started, nice and slow. I began feeling that stuff. That sound got inside me and moved all through me. I thought, "This is where I'm supposed to be." Willie would stand with his trumpet, listening. You could see his foot tap on the one. I wanted to try to please him, because I wanted to join that band. I found out one way. The Lord told me, "Watch his foot. If his feet move, he's listening. If it ain't moving, you have to make it move." That's how I learned to stay on the one.

Willie relaxed me by being where he was. I picked up the vibe off him. I slowed down, stayed where Willie wanted me.

He accepted me into the band right away, and we recorded right away and went out on the road soon after. I couldn't have been happier.

Musically we all fit perfectly. We learned to stay out of each other's way, and how to groove. Willie taught me about being in the pocket, taught me about the rocking chair—he'd tell me "put it in the rocking chair!" I could see him sitting back in the control room, looking like he's in a rocking chair on a certain beat.

When I first got to Hi Records, the music business had started changing. Bill Black had played upright bass for Elvis Presley at the beginning of rock 'n' roll. After that, Bill had a bunch of instrumental hits with his own group, the Bill Black Combo, recording for Hi. Ace Cannon, another white musician, had recorded instrumental hits for Hi. The atmosphere there was mixed, because the company had a black producer, Willie Mitchell, but mostly white with white groups showcased.

Willie had brought some black musicians in to record with Bill and Ace. Al Jackson Jr. played drums on some of those Bill Black Combo hits, because he'd already started working in Willie's band when Willie took over the studio at Hi. My mentor Mr. Able had been there recording with Ace Cannon. He said funny things about everyone, Mr. Able. When I interviewed him for this book, he said, "Ace Cannon was NOT an alcoholic. He was not a drunkard. He just carried around a bottle of whiskey with a straw in it."

When I showed up to Royal studio, I saw this big upright bass in the corner. It sat there for years. Leroy never fooled with it. I wondered about it and asked. Willie Mitchell told me the bass had belonged to Bill Black. He played that on Elvis's records. By the time I came around, Bill had died. That bass let me know nothing lasts forever.

But the run we had beginning in 1967 and lasting over ten years felt like it couldn't be stopped. And we made music that will go on past our own days on this earth. Willie had the vision to bring in O.V. Wright, Ann Peebles, Al Green, Otis Clay, and Syl Johnson to sing. But the one constant on all those records is the Hi Rhythm Section. There are some great studio bands out there, but I don't know any that could hang with us hit for hit, style for style, playing live and recording.

The Hodges brothers were the core of the band. Teenie on guitar, Charles on organ, Leroy on bass. Archie "Hubbie" Turner, Willie's stepson, played organ also. He was in Vietnam when we started, but he got back by 1970 and was a part of the band after that. Those Hodges boys came up in the country, Germantown, outside Memphis. Their father Leroy Hodges Sr. led a band called the Blue Dots, where they all learned. They also had a guitarist named Earl the Pearl in that band. He taught Teenie, and he's still around today. Hubbie was in their band and brought them to Willie's house.

Teenie went to live with Willie. That was the first piece of the puzzle Willie put together. He groomed the guitarist and made him one of the geniuses of rhythm and blues. Leroy came in next and they brought in Charles. The brothers had chemistry.

Willie wanted to build an empire of music. He knew it started with musicians who had their heads in the right direction. As hungry as we were, as funky as we were, shit, we put everybody in the charts.

The first session I played at Royal Studios with the Hi Rhythm Section wasn't for Hi Records. Don Robey, who owned the Duke, Peacock, and Back Beat labels, brought a singer named O.V. Wright in to record. Robey reminded me of Sunbeam Mitchell. He came to record and do business, he didn't play. O.V. did "8 Men 4 Women," which came out in 1967. I think of O.V. as the finest vocalist I ever worked with. I loved him from the top.

Willie Mitchell said to pay attention to the story in a song. I understood. It's like our artists were singing to the world about our problems.

What O.V. sang always related to my life. His songs got me through. "Nickel and a Nail," is incredible. Willie felt like if he'd lived people would recognize O.V. as the greatest singer in the world.

O.V. had his demons. He and the Hodges brothers went back a long time and some of the people they hung around, Arthur Brown and Sugar Man, were into drugs. I saw what happened around the studio and found out that Arthur Brown was O.V. Wright's dealer. When he couldn't get O.V. one thing, he'd bring Robitussin. I saw O.V. drink a bottle of syrup for a session. He took his shirt off and started sweating. But his voice rang out clear as a bell. I never wanted to be that way, I wanted to be natural.

My first recording for Hi Records was for Willie Mitchell, on his version of King Curtis's "Soul Serenade." Charles Chalmers played the saxophone lead. He later became one of the house back-up singers in Rhodes-Chalmers-Rhodes.

"Soul Serenade" became a hit in 1968, and we took off almost instantly. That record got us booked into some great shows thanks to a married couple who ran a booking agency, Donny Dortch and Bettye Berger.

Leroy lent me twenty dollars when we left to buy burgers or whatever when we stopped. I never will forget that. He said, "This'll help you when we stop. Just pay me when you can." We got real close from that. The Hodges brothers all had heart. Willie had his brother James with us, and Don Bryant, who'd worked with Willie for a few years and fit in like a brother. I needed a family and they were a family.

We went to film the *Midnight Special* TV show in Los Angeles. We were going to do Joey Bishop's show, too, and we played with Ike and Tina Turner at a club called the Haunted House. We ended up recording Ike and Tina's record "The Hunter" after that. Tina got nominated for a Grammy on that one.

Willie and the band played Disneyland at night. We performed Willie's instrumentals, "Bad Eye," "Grazin' in the Grass." After that, Don Bryant came out to sing a few numbers. We filmed *American Bandstand*. I saw that show. I don't know if we were on any of the other shows we taped.

I learned from Willie all the time. He said when we perform live to pay attention to the audience. Look for a foot patting under the table, a hand clapping, tapping fingers on the table. He would walk around stage and clap to see how the sound moved from different places. Because of what I learned from Willie, when I perform or play I listen for the acoustics. After playing in white clubs, I knew how to play softly but well.

The night we played the Troubador, Faye Dunaway hit on me. I didn't go with her. First time there, I didn't know nothing about California. I didn't know who she was, even though this happened shortly after she starred in *Bonnie and Clyde*. I saw those two damn bodyguards with her. She liked me, and I was flattered, but I had to be careful. Maybe the only time she's been denied. But I was afraid, not knowing my way around Hollywood.

We were staying at a hotel, and I saw Sly Stone get out of his limousine and walk through the place smoking a joint like he's smoking a cigarette. I had never seen someone smoke dope like that before, in the open. I saw how fast the town was, what was going down in it.

Me and Leroy Hodges, who I call "Flick," went to the Whiskey A Go Go to see Junior Walker. We met the guy there who played Linc Hayes in *The Mod Squad*. He said, "I'm just here to see Junior Walker, would you mind if I hang around you guys?" I said, "Yeah, Junior is our favorite." He sat at the table with us, nice guy.

After my daddy Leroy Grimes left Memphis for Michigan, we had kept up. He liked what I did with my life. He used to ask me, "Do you know Junior Walker?" He said Junior Walker was his neighbor in Battle Creek. He said they'd hang out and talk about me. The morning after we saw Junior Walker perform at the Whiskey, his bus pulled up outside the hotel. I told Flick, "I'm gonna try to get on."

The bus driver opened the door and Junior was on the bus. I introduced myself, asked to speak to Mr. Walker. The driver let me on. I walked down that narrow aisle and saw him—Junior Walker sat on the back seat with a bucket of Kentucky Fried Chicken. He had a drumstick in his hand. I told him he and my daddy were neighbors. He said, "Yeah, he's my card buddy. I know him real well." He shook my hand, said, "You're doing great work," and I got off the bus.

Things were happening in L.A. Bobby Womack came and took us out to the beach. He and Teenie were like brothers. We stayed near the Hollywood Palace. You could walk out the hotel, look down the street, and see the Capitol Records building. That was the beginning of my life to see these places.

Even after all of that action, the best was yet to come. In Los Angeles I reunited with my twin daughters, Ann and Jan. They were happy to see me and I felt the same. That was the greatest time of my life. Willie gave me some money to give to the girls. I had just joined the band so I hadn't earned much yet. Willie gave me two hundred dollars, a hundred for each of them. I've never forgotten. The girls were twelve, and very pretty. We felt great to be together, but there was a little incident.

The dude who married their mama tried to start something with me, so I had to get away from there. He thought I had come back for his woman. I was just there for my children. We had to make arrangements to visit at my hotel. We got together again but just didn't have much time together because of that man getting in the way. I found out later that he had broken the girls' mama's arm and leg over this.

That situation messed me up for years. I've wondered what my girls thought of me, because I don't think they know how they were taken from me, and how I felt about them. I didn't want to cause them or their mama any trouble, and as hard as it was, I stayed away from them. I would love to sit with them and tell the whole story. I was made to feel like their mama and grandmama just wanted me out of the picture. Messed me up for a long time.

It almost didn't matter. After we left L.A. we were set up to play gigs all the way back to Memphis. The van we were traveling in blew two tires and rolled three times. James Mitchell was thrown through the windshield. As the van rolled the third time, I saw a tractor-trailer coming and thought this was it. But the van had gone to the shoulder and stopped. It so happened, doctors who were getting off work stopped their car and ran across the highway. They told us to sit tight while they called an ambulance. We was all laying out on the highway.

Willie Mitchell broke his ankle. Don Bryant broke his nose. Me and Leroy weren't injured. Somehow, it got back to Memphis that we were all dead.

We were going to play an Air Force Base. We still did the show. When the people all saw us come in, they gave us a standing ovation. Willie came in with his ankle in a cast. Don Bryant came in all bandaged up. The doctor told James not to play his horn, but James played anyway. Don Bryant sang with his nose broke. His nose would bleed.

That wasn't the end of the tour, or the end of the excitement. Another big one hit us before we made it home.

CHAPTER NINE

At a club in Waco, Texas, we saw this guy walking around with an overcoat on. His hair stood up on his head. Stars were wearing processes at that time and he needed his fixed. All the people in the club ignored him. We didn't know who he was. He came up on the bandstand and told Willie, "I'm Al Green. Can I sing a song?"

We knew Al Green had a record called "Back Up Train," but I didn't know of anything else he'd done.

Willie told him, "You ain't no Al Green. I don't let anybody sing on my show."

During our break, Teenie told Willie to ask the club owner if that really was Al. The man said it was. Willie asked, "What happened to him?"

Willie was looking for a major act—that one voice. So it didn't hurt to give this guy a shot. Willie decided to let him sing.

Al walked out on stage. He showed us what to do, just wanted us to vamp the song. He said to me, "I don't want you busy. Just give me that rim shot." He was putting the shit in place. I could feel him. He went out there. Opened up his mouth, "Back up train..." The whole fucking house went up. After the show we brought him backstage and Teenie talked to Willie. They asked Al to come down to Memphis.

Al first stayed in a house in Orange Mound. The place had no furniture, but a shoebox full of reefer.

Not long after we got back, Dr. King was assassinated in Memphis. I knew this town was bamboozled. There were too many people toting rabbit foots. When I asked why they'd do that, people told me a rabbit foot brings good luck. I knew that was a lie. I've heard too much of the scriptures.

We were in the studio with Al Green when we found out. When Dr. King was assassinated and the word came to Willie, he told us what had happened. He said, "The streets are getting locked down. You got to be off the streets. We've been permitted to stay on to work."

Everybody was so hurt Willie called off the session. We heard that people could go to work and go home but the streets needed to be clear. We were under curfew. Fire trucks, ambulances, police were everywhere outside. The National Guard came out. It was amazing to see all of these men working to calm the city so that nothing would go down. Those soldiers were out there and they weren't bullshitting.

When I got home, I couldn't hear a sound. There was so much peace. God has given me the power to tune everything out, but I'd never heard such silence.

I visited a man named Mr. Hildebrandt who I always told the news of the day to. He was sitting outside. I told him what happened. We saw a pigeon on the sidewalk. It didn't look hurt. It just stood there. God told me to go get it. When I stuck my hand down, the pigeon pecked me. God said, "Don't let that worry you. Go on, get it." I picked up the pigeon. It walked up my arm and stood on my shoulder.

Mr. Hildebrandt smiled and said, "That's a good sign, Howard. A pigeon's right next to a dove. God got his hands on you."

At the studio, we constantly worked on our sound. If you listen to Willie's "Soul Serenade" and Al's "I Can't Get Next to You" it doesn't sound like the same group, but it is, just two years apart. I got a black Rogers set at Royal studios. All the Hi hits were on that set. Al Jackson played it too. I used to sit with Willie working on the drums all day. An old bass player named Robert McGee taught me how to tune my drums. Willie said, "Ain't nobody tune a drum like Howard."

Before each session, Willie would say, "I don't want nobody in the studio but Howard." We worked two hours on the sound. He'd want the toms half-dead, with no overtones. When I'd hit it, "boom" and it's dead. No reverb. No booooom. He said, "No, I don't want that shit." So I learned from what he heard. He'd get every piece of the kit tuned exactly as he wanted. Sounded pretty good to me, too. Drum heads loosen up, so before each track, he'd sound check the drums, make sure they were still there. Might have to adjust a little. My cowhides didn't go too far out of tune.

When he heard what he wanted, he said, "Don't touch the motherfucker, come on out. Session time." He'd go get Teenie and his brothers, and everything was on. The drum sound and the bass sound were most definite. Teenie played rhythm, Charles played chords, and Hubbie was free.

Willie said, "I cut you hot, I cut all the pots open on you. When you play, I don't want to miss anything." That meant he had all the microphones on for my track.

According to Willie, my bass drum was the best. That's how he nicknamed me. At one session, he said, "Listen at that foot. When a bulldog get mad, you hear him knockin' over shit, he don't want to be bothered. I can hear you comin', Howard, I know when you're comin', you put that foot down and clamp on that beat." After that, I was known as the Bulldog, or usually just Dog.

Learning to listen pushed me forward. In the club I had to avoid playing too loud. I could do more the more I heard every-thing else. That lesson helped me grow at Hi. When we worked on a song, I laid in the cut to listen to what people had. I held time while everyone's putting the song together, but I kept listening and my mind worked on what else I'm going to do. I knew Willie would wonder what I'd do. The Lord told me, "Give that time to them before you move." I set that time on them and could hear the fills and the way they were creating.

My head was always wide open, looking for that right rhythm. I listened to Teenie, because Teenie was always very creative with rhythms. I could hear ideas for myself in the way Teenie played guitar. Charles would start fooling around off of Teenie, and Willie was back there listening to everything the whole time. I just fooled around, waiting for Leroy, because I want to hear what he's got. Once I heard what he was doing, and he heard what I was doing, that sucker started gelling, coming together.

Willie would sit there listening and then he'd laugh. "Heh-heh, boy, Goddamn, that's it. Dog, what you playing now? Keep that shit. Leroy, I like what you're doing, don't move that motherfucker." We had it and we went at it. When we went at it, we went for the money.

Willie said, "Let's roll this motherfucker! Right now, we got it. Roll the one, Dog, take one!" That's the way he did it. Willie overdubbed each instrument and we had it in less than twenty minutes. They were great guys to play with, so gifted.

I was happy to do these things with them. I just didn't like that I didn't make money. That's the only thing that bothered me.

Things happened around Hi that I didn't understand. Since the Hodges brothers had practically grown up with Willie, that left me a little outside. Teenie was already the head honcho. I saw Teenie and Leroy messing with Willie's girls, "Hey Baby," and all that kind of shit. I wasn't going to do all that to the boss's daughters. I shook their hand, I didn't walk up and kiss them. They all had a personal connection that made me uncomfortable. I just wanted to cut records and go on home.

That personal shit wasn't all I didn't understand. The guys who ran Hi Records were like the mob. Frank Beretta, Joe Cuoghi, Nick Pesce, and John Novarese handled Pop Tunes record shop, Hi Records, Royal Studios, and the jukebox company Southern Music—I used to see their truck delivering records to the cafés in my neighborhood. They recorded the records, played the records on the jukeboxes, and sold them in their stores. It was cool. There never was any violence. They were outstanding guys to be around.

They had a rotten deal set up where they put us on the payroll at Pop Tunes, the record store. I wasn't getting but $106 per week to record all those hits over the years. I had to go to the store and get my check. I didn't sign a contract. Al Jackson was pulling $500 a week at Stax. I didn't get a piece of anything else, and I don't know what the other guys were getting. They had to go pick up their checks too, but nobody ever said what they made. I wasn't comfortable. On top of that, Willie had me paying a kickback. That shows how stupid I was. We were supposed to get $200 per side according to the Musician's Union, but when I got my check for that they made me sign it over and give it back to them. It was the only job I had, and I didn't know what else to do.

When I went to Pop Tunes to pick up my check, they'd be there playing cards, drinking. The store stayed busy up front, selling records. They had a backroom full of jukeboxes and pinball machines. That's where they'd sit back and gamble, have their fifths of whiskey. When they'd see me coming, they'd say, "Hey Howard! Get you a drink."

Frank Beretta was the one with the check. Mr. Cuoghi founded the company, that's how it got the name "Hi" from the last two letters in his name. He stayed jolly and always kept a cigar in his mouth. I kidded him that he reminded me of Mr. Magoo. After Joe Cuoghi died in 1970, Nick Pesce took over. He was a lawyer.

We'd kick it. Mr. Beretta teased me and Leroy about chasing pussy in the street and leaving our wives at home. Upstairs at Pop

Tunes was a long table that would be filled with money. I've never seen so much cash in my life. They had three secretaries there counting, bundling it, bagging it up. They funded DJ conventions, brought together the radio broadcasters, threw them a big party, had drugs, women, everything. They did it to get records played, and it worked.

The money, the profits, were between Nick Pesce, Frank Beretta, John Novarese, and Willie Mitchell. They cut Teenie in and left us out. They made Teenie a writer with Al Green, that's how he made his money. All of us worked those songs. He didn't do more than us to where he could say he wrote the song.

Leroy and Charles got money on the side, but I never did. They started getting new cars, nice houses. I had an old car, and didn't really know what the hell was going on. It had already been organized before I came to work at Hi. They had my goddamn head swimming. In the dark's where they kept me.

I had no time to think, we cut sessions every day. While Willie built up Al Green, we recorded solid hits by O.V. Wright and a singer who Bowlegs Miller brought to Memphis from St. Louis, Ann Peebles.

There was always shenanigans for money at Hi. O.V. Wright worked for years with a writer and singer named Melvin Carter, who cut a version of "Ace of Spades." O.V. came to the studio and heard that song playing and said, "Willie, I like that song. I can sing that song." Willie let O.V. record it and it became a hit, but Melvin and O.V. fell out over that. They had been good friends. Willie later released Melvin's version in Japan—couldn't cross up Don Robey and put it out in the U.S. on top of O.V.

Melvin sang his ass off. He didn't have the name of O.V. Melvin had never sang R&B before. Coming out in 1970, "Ace of Spades" became O.V.'s biggest hit.

Willie's son Horace Mitchell played drums on the road with O.V. Wright. In fact, Hubbie and Horace used to check me out at the Flamingo when I played with Bowlegs. They were the first people connected to Willie who'd seen me and told Willie and Teenie about me.

Horace had to play like the O.V. records I'd cut. I took the time to show Horace. Horace got excited about me teaching him. I liked helping him.

I sat with him and he seemed really hurt. He said he tried to please his daddy, but Willie wouldn't put him on a session. Willie said he couldn't play. That shocked me, because Horace played his ass off. I stopped after work at Peggy's Patio in South Memphis to check him out.

He wanted so badly for his daddy to accept him as a drummer. He ended up getting shot by a woman and ended up in the hospital. It all overtook him and he died.

At the very same time as "Ace of Spades," we had Ann Peebles's biggest hit yet, covering Little Johnny Taylor's "Part Time Love."

Those records were getting more successful, but nobody could touch what we did in 1971. That ended up being the biggest year for Hi, the best year of my musical life, and the worst year of my personal life.

CHAPTER TEN

My wife and I had moved out of her mother's house. I thought that would make things better, but nothing changed.

Willie kept us on the road weekends, so she started bringing home a dude while I was gone. One day, I wanted to get home early and surprise her. Our house had a side door that opened into the kitchen. When I opened the door, she was standing there in a purple negligee, naked underneath, cooking the dude's breakfast. He was sitting right there. He raised up, I dropped my bags in the floor and I slapped him. I said, "Don't you move. I could kill you. I should kill you and her."

I heard God speak. God always stuck with me in these situations. He said, "Let him go. He didn't break in your house. She let him in here. You make it understood to him."

I said, "I'm gonna let you go, but if I run into you any more with my wife, it ain't gonna be this."

Of course it did happen again, and I had to whoop him.

My friend told me where they hung out at—Carl's Lounge. I stopped by on my way to a show at the Rosewood Club. There they were. She's sitting up there in a booth with her legs in his lap. All I wanted to do was to tell her I wanted a divorce. I said to her, "I want to talk to you."

She didn't say anything.

I said, "You're either going out of here over my shoulder or you're gonna walk out."

And he butted in. "She ain't going nowhere."

I reached across him to grab her, and he grabbed me. He jumped up. He shouldn't have done that. I waltzed his butt all over that café. I hit that cat and busted his nose. He was bleeding. Carl, the man who ran the lounge, said, "Howard, y'all can't be fighting in here. I'm a put his ass out."

So, I went out and stood on the sidewalk waiting for him. He got to where he didn't want to come out. Carl grabbed him in a headlock, shoved him out the door, and I grabbed him. When I hit him again, my wife ran past us down the street.

I left. He had bled all over me and tore my ruffled shirt. I went and got a room. The desk clerk thought I'd been shot and called the police.

The police came to my room. The officer said, "Are you hurt?"

I said, "No, sir."

"You ain't shot?"

"No, sir."

"You ain't cut?"

"No. I caught a man with my wife."

He said, "Did you kill him?"

I said, "No, sir."

"Did you whoop his ass good?"

I said, "Yes, sir."

He said, "Good. You should have killed that motherfucker."

He bid me a good night and left. I went over to the liquor store and bought a fifth of whiskey, took a shot, and went to bed.

Going back to my grandfather being a Mason, I've always had people in the community looking after me. While I was having this trouble, a policeman friend of mine came and told me, "We know you're a good man. You don't do nothing but stay at home, keep your yard up, play your music." I didn't know people were paying attention to how I was living my life. They saved me from all the trouble my wife tried to start. They knew I couldn't start the shit she tried to put on me.

My marital problems happened during the time we recorded Al Green's *Let's Stay Together* album. Perfect title for what I was going through. Me and Al Jackson were both having the same trouble, and both working on that album. He was more popular. He had side chicks. I didn't have any, didn't want any woman but the one I'd married.

Al Green could bring stories to life like no one else who's ever sung. It took us a while to understand him. Willie was trying to feel him, we were trying to feel him. Nobody could find Al. Willie cut a bunch of covers, "I Want to Hold Your Hand," and "Summertime." We were learning.

Al and Teenie had started writing songs. They'd get out their guitars at the studio. Al played an acoustic and strummed the chords while he sang. Teenie would listen and jump in. We'd sit around and wait, listening. Leroy wrote out the chords. Willie stayed in the control room, always listening. That's how we first heard "Tired of Being Alone." Hearing that story, and hearing those chords, I knew. Willie didn't like the song. When we started, we fell right in the pocket. That's the hit that launched Hi Records to new heights. After that, everything we touched turned to gold.

In addition to the Hi Rhythm Section, Willie brought in horns for almost every session. I'd worked with Andrew Love and Wayne Jackson, known as the Memphis Horns. I used to see Andrew and Wayne at Stax. Those two horns could verbalize and break down four or five different sounds until they ended up sounding like two more horns. Andrew could make the tenor sound like an alto, and Wayne made his trumpet sound like a trombone. I think they were the key to the Memphis sound. They stood across from each other getting a song together, and they were the ones to figure out the charts. Andrew would say to Wayne, "You take the tonic," and I didn't know what that was.

The Memphis Horns had different members, but Andrew and Wayne were the main duo. They made the Memphis sound huge. They brought up older guys like Mr. Able, Fred Ford, and Gilbert Caple. Sometimes Bowlegs Miller would be involved. James Mitchell, Willie's brother, worked with them. Jack Hale played trombone and Lewis Collins played tenor. Floyd Newman, baritone player, was there at the beginning.

They played on Stax stuff, but also at Muscle Shoals, for Atlantic, for Elvis Presley, and the Doobie Brothers.

When I got in Willie's band, he used his brother James and J.P. Louper on tenor and baritone, and Willie played trumpet. Andrew Love stayed across the street from Hi in an apartment building. One day, Willie needed a tenor player on a session. Bill Ford played that horn for Willie, but he was an alcoholic. And so Willie sent for Andrew even before Andrew went to Stax.

Andrew and I were in Bowlegs Miller's band together. Andrew and Bowlegs used to sit and work out how to play in unison. Andrew on tenor, Bowlegs on trumpet. Well, that's how Andrew and Wayne worked, too.

The Rhodes, Chalmers, and Rhodes back-up singers became part of our sound. You can hear all those ingredients blend perfectly on the title track of "Let's Stay Together." That's Al Jackson on the drum kit. Al Jackson and Al Green co-wrote the song. That's the first Al Green hit that Al Jackson came to work on. Al Jackson ended up co-writing many of the Al Green hits, and I still played on every song.

I could understand why Willie called Al to Hi. What made Memphis music great is just that the musicians all had their own style. At Hi, we worked with plenty of musicians from outside the house band. Willie and Al Jackson had worked together before. Willie trained Al. When Al Jackson came to Hi, I laid in the cut, I stayed cool. Me and Al never had any falling out. In fact, working together on those great records and bonding over what happened to both of us in our marriages made a friendship between Al Jackson and myself.

Al Jackson set everybody straight right there in the studio when they tried to create jealousy over who played the kit. Al Jackson said to them, "Ain't nobody gonna break up my friendship with Howard. I'm telling y'all now, I didn't come to take Howard's job or to take over. I respect this man. Don't expect you gonna break up a friendship with Howard and me."

Al played my beats up-tempo. I stayed in the laid-back groove. Al always has been a mastermind with sound. I saw him one time put his wallet on the snare to muffle the texture. I used tape to mute part of the snare, tighten the head or loosen it, to give me what I want. To get his deep sound, he used the wallet. He loosened the head on top to get a light sound, like he's beatin' a pasteboard box. Under the bottom, it'd be tight.

Willie Mitchell made sure I didn't cop Al, and Al didn't cop me. Willie would sit and listen to me before we recorded, and when I got what he wanted, he kept me there. My sound came from the pitch in his ear.

The songs Al Jackson got credit for he really wrote—"Let's Stay Together," "Look What You Done For Me," "You Ought to be With Me." Al Jackson, Willie Mitchell, Teenie, and Al Green left to Holly Springs to write songs. They stayed in a hotel, wanting to get away from the environment in the studio. They stayed gone a week, a week-and-a-half. Again, they were wrapped up in the clique, and I stayed out. Later, they went to the Virgin Islands and they wrote, "Call Me." Al Jackson created the rim shot based on the rhythms he heard down there.

Willie Mitchell put his foot down and got things how he wanted them to sound. He said Al Jackson was mad at him about "Love and Happiness." Willie said he told Al, "I don't want the motherfucker pretty. I want the motherfucker funky." So, I played drums on that. I would drive the beat, it's a funk thing. Al Jackson played pretty.

Recording that song, we got in a groove and stayed in it. We played it so long, until Willie just got up out of the control room and started dancing. He said, "I got this motherfucker. Y'all can quit when you get ready." You ought to hear the long version of that song. We couldn't get out of the groove.

"Full of Fire" was the same way. I got locked in and Al Green jumped to another mood.

After we cut "Let's Stay Together," Willie said it needed conga drums. I didn't feel it needed anything, Al Jackson sounded so tight. But Willie being such a mastermind knew.

He said, "The conga drums gonna put the balls on this motherfucker." That's what he said. "It's gonna put elephant balls on it."

He took the conga drum out. I got on it. He said, "I want you to play with two fingers. Don't put all your fingers on because it'll bleed in. Let me pull you up in the control room. I want you to play real light."

He mouthed the beat he wanted. I started playing. He said, "That's what I want. Get in the pocket with Al. I want the conga drum to dance."

I thought, "How the hell am I gonna do that?" I remembered a commercial for Budweiser they put out at Christmas with the Clydesdale horses. They'd clop along and their heads bobbed up and down. All my ideas come from commercials and cartoons. I could see those horses in my mind's vision on the beat Willie wanted. I played that sound and Willie said, "That's it, now we gon' cut this motherfucker."

He rolled the tape. He played it back and called me in. Willie said, "It's a monster! It's a motherfuckin' hit! All because of what you played." He took the conga and made it bounce off Leroy's bass line so it blended with everything.

With those smash hits, that gold album, Willie's vision for Hi had come true. Everybody we were working with was hot, we had Hi artists in the charts, solid hits on O.V. for Don Robey, and groups from Westbound Records in Detroit in the charts. The Detroit Emeralds and Denise LaSalle had come down to record with us. With Denise, we cut a monster hit, "Trapped by a Thing Called Love." That was another tune that told my story. We ended up cutting Denise's whole first album.

Bill Coday came to Hi from Chicago, with Denise LaSalle. The time we recorded "Trapped by a Thing Called Love," we cut a Bill Coday number called "Get Your Lie Straight." That song should have been a hit, but it is a classic. The "Get Your Lie Straight" rhythm has a 4/4, backbeat, four on the bass, and a lick on the snare.

When we first cut the Detroit Emeralds, we'd been with Al Green all day and we were packing up. Barney from Westbound Records walked in. He managed the Detroit Emeralds. He said he had one song he wanted to cut. Barney caught us at a good time, we were fired up. Willie agreed to stay and cut it, and we agreed to help him.

Abe Tilmon led the Detroit Emeralds. He was a great guitar player. Abe wanted everyone to play live, together. We usually cut each instrument separately and Willie overdubbed. Abe brought something different. He fed us all our lines from his guitar. He played the drumbeat, played the bass line, and he played the leads for each instrument, all on his guitar. We started playing this song, and he started singing, and that sucker came together in one take. The song was called "Do Me Right." Barney took that record, paid us, and they set up a deal to cut more records with Willie. Their next four records with us all hit the charts, and some went gold: "Wear This Ring," "You Want it You Got it," "Baby Let Me Take You," and "Feel the Need in Me."

Those are some of the greatest songs we cut, and the best music ever to come out of Memphis. People don't even know.

Abe Tilmon wrote those hits about his wife. She broke his heart. He came back to Memphis half out of his mind from whiskey. He died not long after. He was only thirty-seven. Sometimes I feel lucky when I think about my old friends that have gone on. Could have been me.

The trouble with my wife held me up and carried me through those sessions. And that music held me up and carried me through the trouble with my wife. All of those songs are special to me. The words to those songs were all I had to help me understand what was happening. As tough as things got, I found peace in the studio. I sank into my rhythm, where all thoughts stopped. I breathed deeply and let my heart guide me.

This hot time at Hi got us some attention. Atlantic Records made a call to Willie to cut Roberta Flack, Aretha Franklin, and Donnie Hathaway. The deal was set up for fifty grand apiece for us in the group. Jerry Wexler and Tom Dowd had been to the studio a couple times. Tom Dowd had complimented me on my work. The day they came over he said, "I've been listening to you. You do some amazing things on those drums." I said, "Thank you, sir." I could tell being around him that music was his whole life. He talked about Aretha, Roberta Flack, Donnie Hathaway. He was going to come in with Willie to produce them. We thought we were going to do it. We all felt excited about it.

I don't know what happened, something went down. Willie said he didn't want to be bothered with all them crooks. He didn't want them to start running the company. Willie might have known how Atlantic had taken over Stax Records and almost ended that company. He said he had enough artists, and just wanted to keep it like that. He had to know something was up. Willie turned it down. That was our shot. If we had done it, we'd all be rich today.

Some of that work ended up going to Chips Moman at American. I got a chance to see Tom Dowd over there at American. I used to go by and holler at Chips sometimes. They were very successful. Would have been the same way with us. I was looking for that. I was at the peak of my life. It didn't happen. We all felt let down.

❖   ❖   ❖

In November of 1971, Denise LaSalle's "Trapped by a Thing Called Love" was going gold and O.V. Wright's "A Nickel and a Nail" was going strong. We had "Tired of Being Alone" out, and "Let's Stay Together" getting ready to be released. By this time, we felt that no other band on the planet could play so fresh, so original, with so many different singers. I stood at the top of my game, and should have been on top of the world. My relationship held me down.

My wife stabbed me on Thanksgiving night. She didn't want to go with me to see my people. I ended up getting seventeen stitches in my leg. When the police came, I was standing in a pool of blood. Nobody would take me to the hospital. A neighbor brought me to the doctor. I told a lie and said I'd fallen and cut myself on a piece of glass.

The doctor said, "Mr. Grimes, this is a knife wound." I loved her, and didn't want to get her in trouble. The doctor said, "You walked in here this time. Next time, they'll be wheeling you in."

I still didn't leave her. I'm just looking at the woman's big ass, big titties. Not thinking. My mother told me, "That's not the wife for you."

I have to tell this. It's been eating me up for many years. I want men to know.

After she stabbed me, I fell right back in with her. She pulled the same shit on me. I came off the road from playing Carnegie Hall for Al Green. I went inside our apartment. I saw her panties lying on the kitchen floor. I saw her bra lying in the hallway. I'm picking up this shit—her shoes, her blouse. I saw no one in either of the bedrooms. I went through a door that leads to the dining room. Right behind there is a door that hides the hot water heater. She was standing behind there waiting, with a butcher knife. She pushed open the door and got in front of me. Her hair all stood up. She looked like a demon.

"You out with your bitch," she said.

I said, "I wasn't out with nobody."

She charged at me. I picked up a chair to protect myself. She went to stab me. I jabbed her one time with the chair leg, right between the eyes. That knocked her to the floor. While she was down, I whooped her ass. I didn't want to die.

I got tired of almost being killed and divorced her.

CHAPTER ELEVEN

The next song we cut was by Ann Peebles, "Breakin' Up Somebody's Home."

I had no idea that Ann was going to cover that Albert King song. Now that did feel like a competition, because Al Jackson Jr. had cut that. He played drums on Albert King's version. It felt to me like he was challenging me to see if I could do it. I didn't want to rip off Al. When you select a record that's out, you have to do better than what it already is. As we got it together in the studio, the song confused me, but I came up on that rhythm I used to play at Currie's from the Five Royales. All I did was play that, put some air in the hi-hat to draw out a longer sound. I got away from what Al played. I could still hear Albert in my head. I needed to get him out and see what Ann's doing. I watched Willie in the control room. He stopped us and said, "Keep what ya got, but give it some bass drum. Let me hear your foot."

Ann came to us as a young girl with a very nice personality. She laughed a lot. Don Bryant always had her laughing. Her first song, "Walk Away," did okay, but Willie and the band were trying to find her. Like with Al Green, we did covers on Ann, like "Part Time Love" and "I Pity the Fool."

She had two hold-ups, her diction and her timing. People could hardly hear what she was saying on tracks. Her time concerned Willie the most. That's when he put me on timing with her. She didn't know how to get in, where to turn around. I showed her it's almost always four bars at the intro, four bars at the verse. The bridge can be eight bars straight. Solo, four bars, then you sing the tag. You got nothing left to do but jump back to the top, and then hit the tail of the song. All songs were written and recorded that way. I showed her a little beat I played, and she caught on. She got to counting the bars. She learned to hear me turn and once she caught on to that, she'd jump back to the vocal. She stayed relaxed, stayed with the drums, and didn't jump time. Ann Peebles always has had an excellent, soulful voice. That's why Willie jumped at her, and why we worked her up—so much church in her. I love everything I cut with her.

Willie assigned Don Bryant to teach her to sing clearly. Ann and Don fell in love and that led to a long marriage that's still strong. She blossomed through Don. Things really took off. Don and Earl Randle were the Hi Records staff songwriters, and they really got to writing for Ann.

Don deserves a book of his own. Don's a little like I am. After staying quiet for years, he came back and cut two great albums with Scott Bomar in Memphis. I got to play on both. He still sings like a young man, but he goes back farther with Willie Mitchell than anybody else, even the Hodges brothers. Don Bryant led the Four Kings, which were a vocal group that sang with the Willie Mitchell band back in the early '60s while I played with Ben Branch and Bowlegs. Willie Mitchell and the Four Kings mainly played the Manhattan Club in South Memphis, where Elvis Presley had his birthday party just about every year. The club is still there, and the street it's on is now called Elvis Presley Boulevard.

Don had started off as a songwriter with Willie before they even got to Hi. They worked with groups like the Five Royales at Home of the Blues Records on Beale Street. That label started the same time as Stax and Hi and cut some instrumentals by Willie and blues records by Roy Brown, the Five Royales, and some others. That's really the place that taught Willie how to produce records.

Don came to Hi with Willie and became first staff writer under

Willie. It wasn't unusual for him to be placed with Ann. Earl Randle wrote her first hit, "I'm Gonna Tear Your Playhouse Down." Don wrote her smash, "I Can't Stand the Rain."

From Don's lyrics and Ann's vocals, we felt we had a hit. When we cut "I Can't Stand the Rain," the track was tight, but naked. Willie thought it needed something. He's the greatest at layering sounds. I always saw these timbales in the studio, in a guitar case. Willie told me to get the timbale. I'd never messed with them. I took them out of the case and hit them down the line. A commercial came into my mind about a percolator. You could see the coffee percolate. I made the timbale drip like that coffee bubbling up in the percolator. Teenie picked up on the last note and blended his guitar with the timbale. That's what makes the intro. John Lennon called it the best song ever, so I think we got it right.

When I came to Hi in 1968, Don Bryant was the main staff writer but we picked up other songwriters as the business got going. Dan Greer stopped by from time to time. Dan Greer painted the sign for Satellite Records. I saw him out on the ladder the day I went in with Rufus to cut "'Cause I Love You." Willie picked up songs from Dan. He wrote for Wilson Pickett, Arthur Conley, and James Carr.

Songwriter Earl Randle had come to Hi from Indianola, Mississippi. We got acquainted in the writing room. He started telling me about where he's from. B.B. King was about all that had happened there, and all he did was leave there.

Earl told me he wanted to write a song with me. I told him I didn't know how. He said it's nothing but a letter, or a poem. So, we sat down at the piano. We wrote a song called "Steppin' Out." Syl Johnson needed one more number on his record, and he covered it. That's the first time Willie Mitchell accepted something I'd written. So, Willie and I sat and wrote "Sixty Go." I wrote "Willie Wham." They're instrumentals. Earl gave me that opportunity to write. Later, Robert Cray recorded "Steppin' Out." I got more money for that than anything I recorded.

On top of "Tear Your Playhouse Down," Earl Randle wrote "Any Way the Wind Blow," for Syl, and "Into Something (Can't Shake Loose)" for O.V. All are classics—Earl is a poet.

Even though we made such great music, the Hi Rhythm Section didn't get along and we didn't work smoothly. Teenie had already started acting like the star of the show. He caused major problems for me, and Willie just let him. We'd be playing a session and I'd know I needed to finish the session to get my bills paid. Teenie would stop in the middle of the session and say, "I ain't playin' no more. I'm going to California."

Willie asked, "How long you gonna be gone?"

Teenie said, "I don't know. Maybe a week or two."

I said, "Man I need to finish this here." Willie would say, "I can't do anything until Teenie gets back."

They did a lot of shit to me. I had to take it. I constantly was falling, never progressing. Teenie and I stayed at each other's throats.

I asked him, "Why don't you like me? I ever misuse you?"

He said, "Nah."

I said, "How do we get into these things?"

He said, "What the fuck you mean?"

And it started over again.

He had that Ike Turner mentality. And I don't know how much the drugs changed him. He had come up with Ike so he learned that way. Him and Ike were tight. He saw Ike whoop a woman many times. He had chicks strung out on drugs and in love with him.

Teenie always had something against me, I'll never know why. Willie told him he had to change his attitude and quit doing people like he did. Teenie said, "What the fuck you mean? You're the one taught me."

The atmosphere around us could stress anybody. With that success, people expected that we had money. People grabbed at us for power. Snitches were all over the studios and clubs, watching what musicians do in their private lives. They caused a lot of chaos. A lot of friendship was lost. I stayed out of that. I kept quiet. I saw fights break out over things that had been said. Snitches spread talk about who was saying what. Led to a lot of mess. I saw the corruption. It made me stay away. All I would do is come in and cut my tracks, then I was gone. I thought I helped myself by staying out of trouble, but that's what hurt me. I didn't socialize. I never joined the clique.

Musicians were fucking each other's wives, snitching on each other. I didn't want to be in that shit. I knew these people were no damn good. They still started trouble for me with my wife, spreading lies. Al Jackson and his wife were up to their necks in it. Willie Mitchell's brother James went through the same thing with his wife I went through with mine. James Mitchell was about like I am. He came home off the road with the Doobie Brothers and caught his wife fucking a policeman. That fucked him up. He said he stood there a minute and looked at them. He could have killed both of them. He said they were so into what they were doing, they didn't know he's standing there in the door. He just left. James never no more was himself.

Al Jackson carried a camera case everywhere. I asked him why he's carrying a camera when I've never seen him snap a picture. He said, "It ain't no camera." He popped it open and I saw that Luger pistol. I knew he must be in some serious shit. But I knew that if he carried, it's because he needed to.

Outside musicians who came to the studio tried to hip me to what was going on. The drummer Ewell Jones from Motown came down to do some tracks. Ewell saw the whole thing.

He told me, "Howard, there's too much bullshit over here." That's just what he said. "We don't have none of that at Motown. I cut Marvin Gaye upstairs, go downstairs and cut the Supremes." He explained how they operated professionally. "One day I cut the Temptations downstairs, go upstairs and cut Smokey." He saw

Teenie assing off, talking about how he needed to get something to eat, when we were all there to work. Ewell said we wasted too much time between tracks. He said we needed to let the bullshit stay outdoors while we work. Teenie still took all the time he wanted. I'd show up ready, he'd have to fuck around and smoke a joint until I'm drained. I tried to tell Willie and them I'd come to work.

To have those guys from Motown around opened my eyes. I loved their drummer "Pistol" Allen, he's from Memphis, and Leroy always listened to James Jamerson, the bass player. We patterned ourselves after them. Leroy got ideas off Jamerson, particularly "I Heard It Through the Grapevine." I wonder how much more we could have done at Hi if we'd had our shit together on the level of Motown.

The records all sounded so smooth, so tight, so harmonious, you never could have guessed about the chaos by listening. We had so many artists in the charts, more singers started flocking to us. Otis Clay came to Hi in 1971, and after him came Syl Johnson. Both moved to Hi from labels in Chicago. After Syl and Otis had hits, Tyrone Davis wanted to come to Hi. We talked about it, but I told him not to come. We had great artists, great storytellers. But all the eggs were in one basket—Al Green. The other artists' records took off on their own.

Willie played the game properly. He made friends with powerful deejays in the big markets. He made a deal with deejay Al Perkins out of Detroit to cut a record on Al if Al would give Hi heavy airplay in Detroit, a big market for us. Willie made a similar deal with E. Rodney Jones out of Chicago. He was another popular deejay, and a very nice gentleman, but people said he was a gangster. Pervis Spann was another one, powerful deejay, nice man, with rumors that he was a gangster. All them gangsters Willie knew took to me. I didn't know if that was a good thing or not. I did not want to get tied up in that and get knocked out the box.

I think those friendships with Chicago gangsters brought Chicago artists to us. I took Otis Clay out and made him feel welcome in Memphis. He wanted to check the bands. He wanted to see what music made the people respond. We went out downtown to the Music Box and the Flamingo Room. We went to Currie's, my favorite club in my old neighborhood. He didn't want to be introduced from the stage because the women would overrun him and he didn't want that. He wanted to chill out and see what Memphis was all about. Otis Clay knew all of the gangsters, and he filled me in on them.

Syl Johnson came to us after Otis. While we were cutting "Any Way the Wind Blow," Syl said God put the pussy on earth and put him down here to get it. Syl always had crazy thoughts in his head. He makes me laugh. He's a great artist and a great person.

I can see Willie now, sitting in the control room. He usually had a tall glass of straight vodka with ice in his hand. I could see the joy in him. He didn't show a lot of wear from the pressure he felt, but I know it affected him. Willie spent so much time on songs. When we cut them, he'd sit and drink on them all day. He'd overdo it, his ears would get shot and he'd have to get off of it.

When we cut "We Did It" on Syl Johnson, Willie went looking for Darryl Carter. Darryl masterminded hit records. He had written hits for Joe Simon, Wilson Pickett, Bobby Womack. Willie thought "We Did It" wasn't nothing. He wanted Darryl to fix it, and found him at his job in Chicago at United Artists. Willie said he needed help on the record. Darryl said he heard the first note and told Willie, "That's a smash."

The moment Darryl heard my foot and the timing, he knew it would be a hit. Willie wanted Darryl to be a fresh set of ears. Darryl agreed to come back with Willie if he'd record Darryl's tracks with me on drums. Darryl said he wanted that stomp, from the Detroit Emeralds stuff. He said, "If you cut my tracks, I'll come back." Darryl became a staff writer for Hi Records. Things started jumping off.

Many people say that my best beat is on an O.V. Wright tune

that Darryl wrote called "Blind, Crippled and Crazy." That all came together fast on a session. Darryl and O.V. were sitting outside the studio on the step. O.V.'s ex-wife ran a beauty shop across the street. Darryl kidded O.V. about going over there and O.V. said, "Man, I rather be blind, crippled and crazy." Darryl jumped up saying, "that's a hit!" He ran inside and wrote the song.

When Darryl wrote, he'd walk around and sing through the lyrics. I could hear the rhythm in his mouth. I watched how he moved to catch on to the rhythm. I used to watch black and white movies of tap dancers, the Nicholas Brothers, Mr. Bojangles, and Sammy Davis Jr. They mesmerized my mind with rhythm. I studied how they did it with their feet. Tap dancing jumped into my mind. I got more off into the song and the tap dancing rhythm stuck with me.

I messed around with the beat, and Darryl got fired up and said, "Yeah, yeah, that's what I want." He never stood still while writing on a song, he walked the floor. Leroy started putting down the bass line. Leroy listened to me, because we bounce off one another. I heard Teenie get in. That's the way we did tracks, listen to each other and blend. I kept messing around and got strong on the snare and my foot. Sammy Davis and Ray Bolger, who played Scarecrow in *The Wizard of Oz*, would look like they kind of trip when they tap dance. Bolger was so good he'd stutterstep and jump back on beat, and that's what gave me the trip beat on "Blind, Crippled and Crazy." I stumble into it, but it's still on the one. Tap dancers are on the one.

Willie heard all this and said, "Boy, that's some crazy rhythm you got there. I don't even know if they're going to be able to tell what you're playing. But, it's in time. And it's funky."

Don Robey died not long after that song came out, and O.V. left Robey's Backbeat label and joined Hi Records. O.V. should have been a comedian the way he kept us laughing. Everybody loved O.V. He was the kind of man you could sit and talk to and learn from him. He knew so much history from his days as a gospel artist.

He talked about how bad Joe Tex was as an artist. In a good way, how awesome he was on stage. O.V. told stories before sessions and he was always worth listening to. The day Willie got the call Don Robey died, O.V. said, "Dirty dog took my money with him." The whole studio fell out. Willie couldn't do anything but laugh.

Our songwriter Darryl Carter worked some at Stax, too. Great songwriter, he wrote "Woman's Gotta Have It," by Bobby Womack. From what he told me, a man named Johnny Baylor, who managed Luther Ingram, would shoot a pistol if he didn't like something in the Stax studio. I'm glad I was out of there when everyone had a gun on their hip. The situation had gotten bad over there and it was all about Isaac Hayes. Darryl was working on a track and Johnny Baylor came in, shot up the ceiling, and Darryl said, "Man, what's wrong with you? You got somebody in here you want to kill? I'm out of here."

I'd heard about Johnny Baylor more or less through the grapevine. I still kept up with Isaac Hayes when I could, and I knew he'd brought in Johnny and Dino Woodard from New York to be his bodyguards. Johnny just about took over at Stax after that. He intimidated everybody. At Stax, a man named Chin worked as a promoter during Isaac Hayes' hot time. Me and Isaac went to school with Chin. Chin sat up in a hotel with prostitutes, smoking cigars and drinking up all the money he should have been using to promote the records, you know, paying deejays to play Isaac's music. Johnny Baylor had Chin beaten.

I finally got to meet Johnny. He brought Luther Ingram to cut at Hi. Must have been after he shot up the house at Stax. Luther Ingram sang a marvelous hit called "If Loving You is Wrong I Don't Want to be Right." Johnny managed Luther. Johnny had heard about how bad I'd been screwed with in Memphis. In front of the whole Hi Rhythm Section, Johnny said to me, "You made all these sons of bitches money," pointing at Teenie and Willie. Johnny said to me, "I like you. And I don't really take to people." Johnny gave

me his card and said, "I kill for a living." Willie Mitchell sat there
nervous. "If anybody fucks with you, does you wrong, just call me
and give their name."

Isaac Hayes had to have told Johnny about how I'd been
mistreated.

That place got quiet. He said to go on with the session and that
broke things up. I got heated up from that. When Johnny left, Willie
said, "He meant what he said." I thought, "You're about the first
motherfucker I'll tell him about." But the Lord said, "Don't do that.
It'll make you a gangster. You'll be a criminal."

I remember when Isaac Hayes's Cadillac El Dorado hit the
street. He drove down Chelsea Avenue going to his grandmother's
house. He always blew the horn at me when he saw me in the
yard. He stopped and blew the horn. He was showcasing that thing
around. It was the most beautiful car I'd seen in my life. All that gold
jumped out at me. He rolled down the window and said, "Doom
Broom." That's what we called each other. I had a 1970 Oldsmobile
98. I had the baddest 98 in this town. God put the dream of that car
on me.

By then Isaac had gone in too deep. He got messed up with
people, almost out of his mind. Johnny Baylor had fucked up his
books, and still demanded money. Isaac needed help. He told me he
needed a bodyguard he could trust. I only knew the bodyguards at
Currie's, Big Diamond, Baby James, and one guy from we went to
school with, Big Ned—we called him Babylon. He didn't do nothing
but play pool. He looked like the guy who broke Cassius Clay's jaw.
Isaac asked me to go get him.

I went out to the pool hall at Thomas Street and Firestone and
found him. He had no shoestrings. He asked what he could do. I just
said you might have to knock some motherfucker's ass out. He said,
"Is that all?" I said mostly just take care of Isaac. I dropped Babylon
off at Stax. Isaac had to go to Florida and left that night. He stayed
gone for about a week. It was in the wintertime.

When Babylon came back, he dropped by my house. He was leathered down. He had a brown safari hat and a roll of money. Babylon said, "I really appreciate that." He tried to give me something off that roll, but I told him I felt happy to help him. Big Ned hired new people, Roosevelt Green from the Largos, Cliff Dates, and one other to be security. They were so tight. Johnny and Dino wanted to kill Isaac, and Big Ned and those guys didn't allow it.

The threat of death hung around Memphis at that time. It affected musicians, and it touched my family. My brother Carl's wife had put him out of the house. He had gotten drafted, went away to war in Vietnam. He came back and didn't understand how things had changed. Her father got him a job, but he didn't want to do nothing but smoke joints. He quarreled with my mother and told her she ought to go ahead and die. She said to him, "Don't you go before me." That's exactly what happened.

I was staying with my mother. I was leaving for work and she told me to send Carl home. He was up there on the corner. I saw him and told him he needed to go back to the house, mama's looking for him. He said he needed some money to get him some beer. I gave him twenty dollars. He never made it home. He got killed outside the Victory Sundry store.

My other brother Dee Dee was in the streets, and he found out the man that'd shot Carl wasn't really after *him*. Carl was talking to the dude that the killer wanted. There'd been some stuff between them long before that hadn't been settled. The dude Carl was talking to had left Memphis to lay low for almost ten years. He came back, and it just happened Carl was talking to him. The killer saw the guy, and went for his gun. The guy pulled my brother in front of him, and my brother got the bullet.

He laid out there covered up and I think mama must have seen him. The killer told me, "I wasn't shooting at the Grimes family, I'd never shoot at the Grimes family. I wasn't trying to kill Carl." I figured it happened because Carl had told mama to go ahead and die. The Bible said disobedient children shall be shown.

The men in the street respected me. I stayed in the neighborhood after things got good for me. The thugs called me a homeboy. They knew I made my living by my hands and defended me, kept me out of fights.

The Willie Mitchell Band performing after a car wreck. You can see the cast on Willie's foot. HOWARD GRIMES COLLECTION

Me at the kit in the late 1960s. HOWARD GRIMES COLLECTION

The great Ann Peebles at Royal Studios in 1971.
HOWARD GRIMES COLLECTION

That's me, my first wife, and Al Green at the time of his first hits.
HOWARD GRIMES COLLECTION

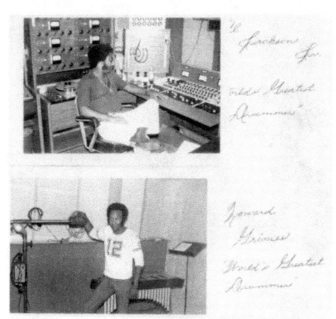

"Al Jackson Jr. World's Greatest Drummer"

"Howard Grimes World's Greatest Drummer"

A page out of an old photo album, showing the two World's Greatest Drummers, Al Jackson Jr. behind the board, and me in the studio.
HOWARD GRIMES COLLECTION

Willie Mitchell and Syl Johnson in the studio, 1971.
HOWARD GRIMES COLLECTION

Our backing vocalists on many Hi Records hits,
Rhodes-Chalmers-Rhodes. HOWARD GRIMES COLLECTION

Me in my Hi Records gear in the 1970s.
HOWARD GRIMES COLLECTION

Willie Mitchell encouraged me to play guitar, but I only ever did it around
the house. That's my pad on Chelsea Avenue in North Memphis.
HOWARD GRIMES COLLECTION

That's me, my old buddy Isaac Hayes, and my first wife.
HOWARD GRIMES COLLECTION

Me, Leroy "Flick" Hodges, and Willie Mitchell in Las Vegas.
HOWARD GRIMES COLLECTION

CHAPTER TWELVE

That's me playing drums on both versions of "Take Me to the River"—by Al Green and by Syl Johnson—the way the rhythm comes off the rim shot to the backbeat, the drive from the foot. I cross cut it—I played half rim and at the bridge, foot and snare. Al Green had written and recorded the song when Syl Johnson said, "I'm a cut this motherfucker, I don't care what you do."

Al felt frustrated by Syl's cover. The band didn't understand it. As crazy as Al Green drove me, I could see how he took it. Did Al not sing it right? It's his song.

Willie had a practice of cutting the same song with different artists. He did that with songs Don Bryant had written for the studio. He did it with O.V. Wright and Otis Clay. But to do that to Al Green, with Al Green's song, just about killed the goose that laid the golden eggs. Nobody talked business to me, so I can mostly guess. I think that the way Willie handled "Take Me to the River" started the end of Hi Records.

The situation began when the *Al Green Explores Your Mind* album came out—October, 1974. We were only a few years in on Al, since "Tired of Being Alone" hit. Things change on you so quickly. This business can tear you up from the top, without any warning.

I never had a bunch of women. I concentrated on being an excellent drummer. Women started coming at me because of Al Green. One night at Currie's, a girl came up to me at the bar. I hooked up with her not knowing. She figured I had money because

I'd cut Al Green's records. I didn't have any money. She was already pregnant. The rumors that she'd messed around with some cats from Firestone came out. They warned me, "She gon' put a baby on you."

She came to my house while I was washing my car. She told me, "If it ain't yours, you're still gonna pay for it." Here's a woman who thinks I'm rich. My mama found out and told me my brother had been going with the woman. The baby belonged to him. That woman got me for child support on my brother's child. I started off paying ten dollars a week to help my brother out and keep things quiet. Willie didn't want any hassles or people causing me trouble where I couldn't think. He got me a lawyer, but it got crazy before it got better. Every record I cut hit the Billboard charts. That gave everyone from girls to the taxman the idea I had money. They didn't ruin me, but they put me in bad shape.

A bunch of excess bullshit had crept in to Hi, too. Al was the key, because that's where the money was. Willie schemed to keep that money in the family. They said Willie's daughter Yvonne was going to marry Al Green. Teenie was talking. He said if Willie got Al to marry Yvonne, that would lock the money down. Al didn't want to do that. All that crap flew over my head, but Leroy passed some of that talk on to me. Willie kind of whispered that Al's a punk. I didn't think that was right, nor any way to treat the man who made the money. I wonder if that situation led to Willie letting Syl do "Take Me to the River." Al didn't want Syl to do it.

There's a song on *Al Green Explores Your Mind* called "One Nite Stand." It's nothing special. Al didn't really give it his everything. But it's another piece of the story about the end of Hi Records.

We were in the studio, cutting more records on Al. On the night everything went crazy, we were working on "Strong as Death." To this day I don't play the record. I had trouble recording it. Al had trouble singing it. Willie had trouble cutting it. I felt uneasy, I couldn't get into it. All the love songs and the happy songs we'd made there worked. Why do something with death?

While we were trying to make something happen with the track, Willie got a phone call in the studio from Ben Whitney. Ben worked on the police force as a detective. He'd been around forever, walking the beat on Beale Street when I first got on the scene. He'd check if I was drinking underage back in the day.

Al Green already had two chicks in the studio. If he wanted anything, he'd pop his fingers and they'd go and get it. Me and Leroy couldn't believe the way Al had them jumping. Ben Whitney brought a third chick down to the studio. Me and Leroy looked at each other when the woman walked in, we knew something was going down.

Al was singing in the booth. We couldn't get that song straight. Willie called it a night. He said, "I think we need to leave this one alone." Al's bodyguard Haywood was there. Al, Haywood and the women all left. I headed home and went to bed.

Leroy called me at five in the morning and said the woman who'd come to the studio was dead, and Al was in the hospital. After that, nobody said too much about it. Al got better, and we went back to work.

When we weren't fussing in the studio, Al and I got along pretty well. We weren't as close as him and Teenie, but he'd rap with me a little. He drove a little green Jaguar at that time. When he headed over to Arkansas to see his people, he'd stop by my house and visit.

One day, he came by. We sat down in the basement and smoked a little reefer. I started not to, but I asked him, "Did you kill that woman?"

He said, "I made a mistake letting that woman in my house. I wasn't thinking. I met her in New York. It was a one-night stand. She was married."

He said he brought her home that night, went upstairs and didn't close the bathroom. The bodyguard and the three women were downstairs. He said he had his back to the door.

He said he felt something hot. That's when she hit him with that pot of grits. He said grits hold heat and they just stuck to him.

He said, "I'm naked trying to get the grits off my back. I heard three shots downstairs. I ran out for my front yard. There was a hole in the wall, a hole in the couch, and hole in the woman."

He said, "Ben Whitney came up in a helicopter. He threw a quilt on me, naked in my front yard, and I don't remember anything after that. I woke up in the hospital."

The woman's husband came to kill Al. They caught him first and told him to take his ass back to New York.

Somewhere in all that mess, Willie let Syl Johnson cover "Take Me to the River." I guess that Willie didn't know if Al could bounce back from all that.

As that simmered, Al took out his frustrations on me. Al couldn't go after Willie. If he went after one Hodges brother, they might all turn against him.

Al walked in to the studio one day and said, "There's gonna be some changes made." His attitude had shifted. "Things ain't gonna be the way they used to be," he said.

I was in the drum booth. We were getting ready to do a session on him. I heard God speak to me, He said, "Ask him who he's talking to."

So, I stepped out of the booth. I said, "Man, who you talkin' to?"

Al said, "Motherfucker, I'm talkin' to you, you fired!"

I said, "You can't fire me. I don't work for you. If Willie says I'm fired, that's it, but you can't fire me."

Willie was sitting in the control room listening. He got up and came out and said, "What's going on? What's wrong?"

I said, "Al Green said I'm fired."

Willie said, "I do the hirin' and I do the firin'."

Al didn't like that. He shut the session down and left. I hung around and Willie called me into the control room. He said, "What's wrong with you and Al?"

I said, "Nothing, not as I know."

He said, "What brought that on?"

I said, "I don't know. He's out there talking. God told me to ask him who he's talking to."

Willie said, "Would you beg his apology?"

I said, "For what? Willie, he has never thanked you or the band for the hits that we give him. He gave us a hundred dollar bonus for a million seller, and Leroy said, 'Keep your damn money, I don't want it.' Al has never thanked you."

Willie said, "That's true. That's right."

I said, "If anything, he owes me an apology for the way he come down on me."

Willie said, "The same way he went up the ladder, he got to come down it. Unless he hang his own neck on top."

I told Willie I wouldn't beg Al's pardon, and I didn't. Next thing I know, Al told Willie to call a drummer named Steve Potts to replace me.

I never had an idea what Al Green had against me. A man named Warren Lewis, a barber in North Memphis, told me I was in a hornet nest. All the sex and filthiness going on at them parties, I wasn't at them parties. The orgies and things they were doing. They'd tell me after they did something that I missed out, but I said "I'm glad I was gone, because that ain't me."

Willie Bean worked as the promotional man for Hi. He took the records out. His job was to get the records on at major radio stations in big cities. He'd make the rounds, drop off records. Great promotion man. He got airplay for Hi. He had married one of Willie Mitchell's daughters. When Willie Bean went out, business was taken care of. He knew everyone in the business. When they had the disc jockey ball, he was there. They had a red door where you could lay up with the hoes. I wanted none of that. I heard Bowlegs and Willie Bean talking about that and stayed my distance.

Bowlegs was the same way. They used to have orgies. Next to Select-O-Hits was a publishing company. They had a studio in back where we rehearsed. Bowlegs used to give late parties over there.

He'd pull in four or five hoes off Thomas Street. They had liquor and weed and all this. They had strippers in one room and orgies in another room. I remember they used to say something about the golden shower. I never heard of that. I said, "What is the golden shower?" Well, that's when they lay down and a woman piss on their face. I said, "Y'all got to be crazy." Musicians were so fucked up in their heads.

I didn't want to be involved in anything they were feeding me, so I stayed away. That's the reason they say I think I'm better than them. No, I didn't want my name dragged into what they were doing.

CHAPTER THIRTEEN

People were scared of Sunbeam Mitchell. He carried a little old pistol in his pocket. He pulled that gun on me back when I worked with his road band. I have never done anything to that man. The business could be so rough and so slow, sometimes you had to work for Sunbeam. He paid you what he wanted to. Might be five dollars and a bowl of chili. That's the reason I didn't much like working for Sunbeam. He always struck me as sad, bored, or angry. If somebody made him smile, he'd do it quick and it cut off. Evelyn Young worked for Sunbeam forever, and she even said, "Yeah, that motherfucker crazy, he ain't got no sense."

Years after I had quit Sunbeam Mitchell's road band—after he'd pulled that pistol on me—I got a call out from Dick "Cane" Cole. He worked at WLOK as a disc jockey and did shows for Sunbeam at Club Paradise.

Out in the street, people were telling me, "Howard, Dick 'Cane' Cole is on the air calling for you to get in touch with him, come to the radio station." I went and turned on my radio and sure enough heard Dick say, "Howard Grimes, if you're out there, come to the radio station immediately."

Nobody had called me out like that before, and I went down to see what he wanted. He was on the air, but he put on some records so we could talk and wouldn't be interrupted. He told me, "Howard, I got Ted Taylor coming in and I need a band. I know you can put it together."

Well, I'd been playing for other people my entire life and never done anything like that. Ted Taylor and the Ovations were on the show. Dick said he'd pay me well, but I said I didn't know if anyone would work with me like that. He told me, "As many records as you've been on, I know you can do this. I believe in you."

Leroy and Teenie wouldn't play with me. I hired two brothers who played bass and guitar. They were bad. I got Hubbie from Hi and Andrew Love and Ben Cauley from Stax to play horns. They all said they'd help me, knowing how many people I'd helped. I told Dick to give me $800 to pay these guys. He said, "I told you you could do it."

The night of the show Ted Taylor came and we sat in the dressing room. That's how I found out he's a black belt in karate. He remembered me from back at Currie's. He'd played there in the '60s when his big records came out. We rehearsed the band. He told me he wanted to take us on the road. He said, "Ain't no band ever played my music as closely as y'all."

Before the show, the emcee Willie Britt came back stage and told me my mentor, Mr. Emerson Able was out in the audience. I went and shook his hand. He sat at a long table with his wife and all of their friends. Mr. Able told me, "You know I got my ear on you, so if you fuck up, I'll know!"

I said, "Yes sir."

Place was packed. Paradise was an enormous club, could seat 3,000 people. With Mr. Able out there, I knew I had to be straight. We played a great show. I waved goodbye to Mr. Able from the stage and didn't see him any more for a long time. Afterwards Dick "Cane" Cole told me, go back to Sunbeam's office and he'll pay you. I lost my breath. I hadn't seen Sunbeam since he had pulled that pistol on me. I felt nervous, wondering what he would do when I come in for the money.

When I went in, he begged my pardon. He said, "Howard I'm sorry I pulled that pistol on you. Would you forgive me?"

I said, "It's all right."

He said, "No, I was wrong."

Well, I knew that but I realized something wasn't working right in that brain up there, the way he treated people.

He laid out $800 in cash. He knew I worked at Hi. He said to tell Willie Mitchell he said hello.

The last time I saw Al Jackson, he told me he was going by to see his wife. He said she had the best pussy in the world. She had shot him before, so I told him not to go there, he didn't know who she had up in the house. He went through the same thing I'd gone through in my marriage. Other men. After all the shit my wife had pulled on me by then, I feared for him.

Leroy called me the next day. He couldn't talk straight to tell me what happened. He just said, "Al Jackson is dead." He said, "Al went to her house. Somebody else was there. Al was found down on his knees like he was praying, begging for his life."

I said, "Man, I told him if he wanted to see that woman, get a hotel room. Don't go to the house. He was so enthused over that pussy of hers."

That messed me up a long time. There's been some strange lies told about Al Jackson. That's why I stayed away from bad people. That's why I didn't hang with them. I'm not going to hell for nobody.

Not long after Al Jackson died, Willie Mitchell offered the Hi Rhythm Section an opportunity to do our own album.

Willie suggested that we cut five instrumentals and five vocalists, different singers. Teenie told Willie, "No, I'm gonna sing."

Willie said, "You can't sing motherfucker."

Teenie said, "Mick Jagger can't sing."

Willie said, "You ain't Mick Jagger."

What Leroy and I wanted was for Ann Peebles to sing a song,

Al Green to sing a song, and fill the album like that. Teenie, Charles, and Hubbie decided they wanted to do the singing. Leroy and I laughed at them. They won.

Teenie was going around people with different musical ideas. He brought in the banjo and did vocals like Steely Dan. That's where his head was. He was in a different world, but he was bringing this stuff to us. On "Black Rock" we used scratching records to highlight the rhythm. That's Hubbie's idea. We were ahead of ourselves. The record came out as funky as anything we ever cut, and more experimental. It shows how much more we could have done with the right set up and encouragement. We needed freedom. That's what we didn't get.

Willie made the record but wouldn't put it out. That's where Teenie fell out with Willie and Pop Tunes. They took the album and froze it. Ten years later, Teenie told me Willie made that call, because he thought if we got a hit on our own, we wouldn't want to cut no more records backing up Hi singers. Willie didn't want to lose the group.

Willie held all of us back. I went along with the shit. I thought other people would hire me. Way after the fact, Willie told me Lou Rawls wanted me to play on his session that turned out "You'll Never Find Another Love Like Mine." Willie said if I'd gone to Lou Rawls' band, they'd have kept me. He said he didn't want that. Willie didn't have the right to do that, but he didn't want to give me up. He didn't own me. He just acted like he did.

Willie's own brother James arranged and wrote strings on everything at Hi, and Willie took the credit from him, too.

Thirty years after we made that record, *On the Loose*, Don Bryant called me and told me to come down to the record store on Beale Street. They had the record. I never knew it had been put out. A label called Demon Records in the UK released it, and the man who runs the record store had gotten some copies on a buying trip.

On the cover, Teenie looks like he has a sandwich in his pants.

He said it was real.

Willie wouldn't let Al fire me, wouldn't let Lou Rawls hire me, but Willie and his partners still sold the company right out from under us without a warning.

In spite of everything, the band still enjoyed making music together, and we still spent most of our time creating in the studio. One day in 1977, we were in the studio getting ready to cut Al. Willie got a call. He said he needed to go to Pop Tunes. He stayed away two-and-a-half hours. We waited on him. He walked in the door, said, "Company's been sold," like he's saying good morning, and went into the control room. From the control room, Willie said, "Everybody got a pension form."

I was in shock.

Willie must have let Al know something was up, because Al hadn't shown up yet. Willie told us that each band member would get a portion of the money from the sale. He said we weren't going to stop working. So, that all felt pretty good. I filled out the form, and later went down to Pop Tunes like I had many times before, to pick up my check.

I thought, "I fed all these people, put them in cars, it's time for the big payback." I figured on getting somewhere around $100,000, just thinking of the many gold records we'd made. Our music made millions of dollars. Even $100,000 seemed kind of cheap.

Nick Pesce had been president of Hi Records since the death of Joe Cuoghi. I met him to pick up my check. Not only did he pay me less than I expected, but he kept his usual kickback. I got around $9,000. I think I'd received a payment of $10,000 but Mr. Pesce kept $400.

I challenged Nick Pesce about this. He snapped. He jumped up and started pushing his desk towards me, like he's going to flip it over. He shouted, "Take your money and get the fuck out of here!"

I love to smile, I love to have a good time. But I caught hell being the nice guy. If somebody says something sideways, I may have to let them know I am a man. But I don't jive. When people misuse me, I wait for my victory. I left Nick Pesce's office. I needed my job and thought that shit would blow over. I stayed there all those years until they made all that money, and then they decided to make that switch.

Even though Willie said Hi Records would stay like it had been, everything changed. The first thing they changed was the drummer. Even though Willie had a perfect formula for hit records, he mixed it up. After giving up the best years of my life and cutting so many hits, I was out. The move never panned out for Hi either. They were through cutting hits.

CHAPTER FOURTEEN

My house was all I had left. No wife, no job, no income. I had no future. The death of Hi Records began my crisis.

I'd go in the backyard and cry, pleading to the Lord. "Why me? What did I do wrong?" He always says the same. "I told you—you obey me well, I'll send you back up." He reminds me.

I stayed in touch with Willie Bean, record promoter for Hi. He didn't like what was going on either. He said to me, "They ain't got nothin' goin' on over there. No sound."

My lights got cut off at the house. I didn't have anything to do but lay in bed with the Bible. With no light and no TV or stereo, I could hear everything going on like never before. I heard ambulances. I heard police. I heard pistol shots and arguing.

The Lord told me, "The Devil has everyone so busy. You've got to understand that you have to put me first. Your shield has to always be up. Your ears have to be able to hear."

I got used to the darkness. It didn't bother me. I could hear God reading that Bible to me. I heard who He was, how He created the earth. I heard Him say He made man from the dust of the earth, breathed in his nostrils and made man a living soul. I said to myself, "That's how it is, so we're dirt." That made sense.

A lot of things started coming together. I forgot all about the world outside. I found out who I was. The more I followed that book, the more it came alive. When I got to the point in Ecclesiastes when He says, "Absent in the body, present with the Lord," I drifted off. I didn't know that I had died. There wasn't anything there.

I don't know how long I was out before I woke up. I felt dizzy. I looked at my hand and touched myself. I said to myself, "I died. Who would believe that?"

I got up. I went in the bathroom and looked in the mirror. I saw His face over mine. I stepped away, and said, "Whoa, what was that?" I went back to look a second time. I could see the thorns on my head. I was born again—He lives in me.

After that, I couldn't put the Bible down. I was poor as a snake but I was full in my heart. The light was there.

He sent my wife to me, who'd caused so much trouble. He told me, "I don't want you to say one word, just listen at her."

We'd been divorced for five or six years. I was sitting at the dining room table. She looked at me and started crying. She saw the outside life of me in the world. She hadn't seen the eternal life in me, because I was so thin. From the world, I looked like it wouldn't be long before I was gone. She didn't know I had been resurrected.

She said, "God told me to ask you if you would forgive me."

I said, "I forgive you. I forgave you when you walked out that door and left me."

She couldn't look at me because I was so poor. She said, "I tried to satisfy two men—one in the street, one at home." She confessed everything she had done wrong. A load fell off of me. She said, "I know that you are a good man."

When she left, I thought of how God said he makes your enemies your footstool.

One day God sent me over to the studio. I didn't want to go. I wasn't working, but I was born again. God wanted them to see they hadn't beat me. He said, "I want them to see the new you."

I went. Willie had an eight-track recording machine on the first floor where we cut our hits. He had another board built upstairs. He never got out of there what he got off the first floor. When I went, they were upstairs.

Al Green and Teenie were sitting there. Willie looked at me, said, "Hey Howard," and looked away. Teenie and Al didn't say anything. I stayed maybe fifteen or twenty minutes. I had no money, no job, no income. I only had Jesus. I had that light on.

There was a husband and wife in the studio dressed in white. I never met them, but I gave them my testimony. They were saints.

As I left, God told me, "Ain't going to be no more hits coming out of here. You're the hit maker. When you asked me to be one of God's great drummers, I gave it to you."

On a stormy night, with lightning and wind, somebody knocked at my door. I didn't have any power on and my only light came from candles. I answered the door and saw Al Green. Right out front he'd parked his white Cadillac El Dorado convertible. He stood there in a white suit, holding a black briefcase.

I couldn't believe it was him. I asked him in. He didn't look too pleased about traveling in that storm. Al stepped into the house and laid that briefcase down on a table. He opened up the case, took out some cash, and set the money on the table. He said he'd brought me $500.

I asked who told him to bring me the money, and he said, "I'm only following instructions."

I don't know if God ordered him or Willie Mitchell did. I told him I couldn't pay him back. I feared that this might be some kind of set up. I never understood that world and had been put through so many trials I got suspicious. I didn't want him or somebody else to come back for the money and hurt me. I told Al that my life is more important to me than having the lights on.

When Al left I got on my knees and asked the Lord. The Lord said, "Do what Al said. Go pay your bill and get your lights turned back on."

To this day, he hasn't asked for that money back.

Leroy, Charles, and Teenie didn't come around. For them to do me like that hurt. After all those years of working together cutting records, traveling, it bothered me for a long time. Hubbie always hollered at me, though, and we're tight to this day.

While my spirit grew whole, the rest of my life still suffered in chaos.

My brother Edward "Dee Dee" Grimes was buddies with Tee Richardson, a clothing designer. He made jean suits with the patches—it was bad. My brother and Tee were trying to help. They said they knew this preacher in Mississippi who could do something. They took me down.

I saw this little white shotgun house. I saw all these people walking like zombies. I was skeptical. I had God with me, and I knew He was putting something on me because I was clean out of my mind. Things were happening in my body, but I couldn't put my hand on what was wrong, all I wanted was to get rid of it. I wanted it out. I wanted to know why I was being treated this way, why I was in this position.

In the house I had to take a number. I got seven. I saw these old women sitting in the house wearing white dresses like nurses. They had on brown cotton stockings and they had on dark shades. They didn't look too happy to see me.

Then I heard the Lord speak. He said, "Don't be afraid of them. These are demons. You're in the house of the devil. But don't be afraid."

I sat there waiting for them to call my number—seven. In the Bible, that is the day the Lord rested. He'd seen everything and it was good. So I knew that was a good number. When the witch doctor called me up, they had tin cups, some green, yellow, burgundy. He had a green one on the table, and when I sat down the table looked wet. That green tin cup started moving towards me. I knew I was someplace I didn't need to be.

He said, "Mr. Grimes, put your right hand out." I put it out. He said, "Turn it over." I turned it over. He took his thumb and put it on my palm. I guess he was feeling my pulse. He held it there a minute and said, "Mr. Grimes, you're steady as a rock." He said, "Everything you been through, you supposed to be dead. Or crazy. Everything gonna be alright. They all been down here, Willie Mitchell, Al Green, Staples Singers. But I like you."

I felt good. He gave me a pouch. It was red on one side, and gold on the other. He told me when I'm out in the street to put it on the red side, when I'm at the house, put it on the gold side. He gave me some medicine that cost $75. I didn't have that much. My brother vouched for me and I got it. He said take a teaspoon every day and it'd solve my problems.

Back at my house, I took a teaspoon of that shit and something happened inside my stomach. I started seeing things. I said, "Something here ain't right."

Then I heard God say, "Pour it out. You don't need that, only thing you need is Me."

I did pour it out but that teaspoon made me sick. I laid out in the hallway and asked God to spare me and give me another chance. I laid down and when I woke up I felt sweaty and weak. I saw where I'd puked and thought, "That came out of me?"

I went out and when I carried that pouch the police stopped me and took me to jail for warrants—child support. I didn't know what the hell was going on. I realized I had a curse on me. It came from that man, Reverend Johnson, in Drew, Mississippi.

They brought me in court and the judge asked the guard to search me. He reached into my shirt pocket, pulled his hand out and hollered, "Get it away from me, get it away from me!" He'd gotten hold of that cursed pouch. That tickled me.

I don't believe in that stuff. I was fucked up and desperate and didn't know what else to do.

I got through the mess. My faith was the only thing holding me. I stood on it and that's where I stand today. My mother used to say, "Every tub sits on its own bottom."

Tee Richardson told me when we were going down to Drew, Mississippi, "Howard, you're gonna see power!" That's what he was talking about, the way that policeman's hand jumped off the pouch when he found it in my pocket.

They locked me up. I stayed in jail three days. I didn't eat. They let me out on Easter Sunday morning. I walked out in the rain onto Poplar Avenue. Went all the way up Thomas Street to Jackson to Bellevue, down to Firestone to Breedlove, to my mother's house. Nobody stopped to give me a ride. I didn't feel too lonely, knowing I had God with me. After three days I needed a shave and a bath. My mother took me in and fixed me dinner. She felt outraged.

She said, "After all you did, with Rufus Thomas, Al Green, Willie Mitchell, none of them help you."

I said, "Mama, it's some things you don't understand." I could have talked. But I always heard a voice say, "They gon' kill you." Something told me I'd have my chance and I would get the last word. All those years I stood with my faith.

Someone called my mother's house when I was eating there and said, "Police done kicked your door in." I went and saw my furniture out in the street. The police were there.

I had run out of money. I was homeless, sleeping in my car. I hated Willie, Al, and even Rufus. They had taken advantage of me. The Holy Spirit kept telling me, "Just play." That's what I did. I continued to play. Played in the juke joints with Earl the Pearl. I just played. I slept in my car before my mama invited me to her house. I rode around all night, sleeping under bridges. People laughed at me. I never stopped. James Harper, who played trombone with Ray Charles, said they can take your furniture but they can't take your talent. The big bandleader in the sky knows all.

CHAPTER FIFTEEN

After that happened, my songwriter friend Darryl Carter took me to Al Green's church. Al had his conversion around the time of my rebirth in the late '70s. He started up a church called the Full Gospel Tabernacle, where he still serves as minister. We got in and saw Al standing in the pulpit, preaching to the people. Al saw us and stopped preaching. We went all the way to the second row. Al walked out of the pulpit. He stood in front of me, rocking. Tears were coming down. I felt confused, I wanted to know what Al's crying for. Al embraced me like Paul did Jesus. He stepped back and looked at me, crying and rocking. He turned around, went back up the pulpit, and he told everybody in the church, "You see that man over there, he's my drummer. He's on all the major hits." He went through all of the artists I'd cut, told the whole house, and went back to his sermon.

After church Al Green invited me and Darryl back to his office. He invited me to come to his recording studio and see what I could do. He tried to give back to me.

Darryl came out and said to Al, "Howard needs a car. Why don't you give him one of your cars out there?" Al never did respond. That upset Darryl, he said Al could give me a car he wasn't using and write it off on his taxes. "Everybody over at Hi done you wrong," Darryl said. "But God got something for 'em."

Al called me to his studio. He didn't pay me, but he gave me an opportunity to do something for myself. He asked if I'd thought about cutting. He invited me to his studio to see if I could cut something.

I took Larry Lee to play guitar. My keyboard player named Blue. James Price played bass. Andrew Love, Wayne Jackson, Jack Hale, and James Mitchell made up the horn section. I put down these tracks. I told them I had no money. They said they owed me for helping out so many people. Andrew said he wouldn't leave me hanging. That's the first time I met Mother Green. Al told her, "This is the drummer on all my records, Howard Grimes." That was the first compliment I'd gotten. She told me, "Son, you're going places." William Brown produced me and gave me the masters.

After all I went through with Al and because of him, I can't say he didn't try and do for me what he could. Another man who never turned from me was O.V. Wright. In 1979, O.V. took me with him to perform in Japan.

During the years of recording hits in the studio, I'd barely played live. After our wreck on the road in 1968, and once we started making money on records, Willie didn't allow us to play out. I played a few gigs with Al Green back then. In fact, he took us to Carnegie Hall on his first hit. I had set up a deal to play Hi artists at Currie's when O.V., Otis Clay, Ann Peebles, and Syl were all under contract.

O.V.'s ex-wife sang on "Eight Men and Four Women." They divorced, and it kind of was leaking around that O.V. had met a schoolteacher. I got to know her, very nice lady. The police rode him all the time, arresting him for child support. Willie would get him out of jail. We were playing Currie's, and the police arrested him right off the stage in the middle of his show. It was embarrassing. That's the way it was here. Behind that, he got deeply involved in drugs. That put him in the hospital. Willie Mitchell paid for him to rehab and get cleaned up to perform and tour. O.V. got straight for that. But when we got back his drug buddies trapped him and he went back to that habit. That's the way he died.

But that trip to Japan was a highlight. I didn't want to get on that plane. I had never flown. That plane went right over the ocean. I read the chapter in the Bible about casting out demons. That flight got choppy and when I said "get the devil out" the plane leveled off and we had no more bumps.

The journey was worth every bit of stress. Japanese fans loved O.V. I felt blessed to go along with him, get some food in my belly, money in my pocket, and a roof on my head.

O.V. got to drinking one night. They left a fifth of whiskey in his hotel room. He didn't let it sit there. At the gig that night he wasn't himself. He come out there on stage with house shoes on, standing up there singing.

After the show we went back to the hotel; he was wasted. Leroy and all of us were in O.V.'s room. Another bottle of whiskey had been put in there. I saw a guy go in the restroom and never saw him come out. I wouldn't leave because I knew some guy was in the restroom. I started to hit the bathroom door, and yelled, "Hey man, everybody's getting ready to leave, you gotta come out." He opened the door and came out.

Something told me to stick around and talk to O.V. for a minute, try to get his head in line. I said, "O.V. I ain't tryin' to run your life, but we're over to represent the Memphis sound. The word will get back to the U.S. before we get home that we're not doing a good job. Man, Willie ain't gon' like that. I don't want Willie mad at me or the band because of your behavior. If you're gonna drink, do it after the gig, don't drink before. You make us all look bad."

He listened to what I had to say. He didn't get angry. I said, "I coulda left you here. There was a dude in your restroom. In the shape you're in, I didn't want to leave you, because I really didn't know what he was up to." I never figured out what that dude was up to, but with O.V. being wasted, I needed to make sure his room was clear. So, I sat there and talked to him. He started listening and looked like he shaped up. "You're the star," I told him. "We don't need bad reports going back to Memphis that you're over here fucked up."

He said, "You're right. I ain't drinkin' no more on this tour."

And he didn't.

Right in front of me there, he started to cry. "Nobody have ever thought enough of me to do what you did," he said. I said, "Man, I ain't did nothin', we all in this together." O.V. never forgot that, and the rest of the tour, we set that place on fire.

O.V. died two years later. By the end, Willie had to carry him into the studio to do his sessions. O.V.'s brother Eddie Wright had a little shop on Brown Avenue, North Memphis. I took him one of the magazines that came out about our Japanese tour. He sat there in his wheelchair and cried. I played with Eddie's gospel group in the church across the street from his place. Leroy played with Eddie, too.

CHAPTER SIXTEEN

Back when things were going strong, I used to have a German Shepherd. I'd play with it outside and notice this woman drive past and blow the horn at me. One night I met her up at Currie's. She had on some white hot pants and black boots. Leroy and I were standing at the bar with Mason Currie, and she walked up and asked me to buy her a champagne. I said I would, but she told me, "I'm joking, I don't drink." After my divorce, I didn't want to study any woman. But I took her number.

She walked off and Leroy said, "That's you, boy." I argued with him about it. She came back to Currie's another night with her sisters. I went over to her table. They were all excited to meet me. We all got along. That's when I had the gold 98, the baddest car in Memphis. She asked me to take her home, and I did, but I never saw her over the next ten years.

After everything else had fell apart, I was living with my mama, making no money. I still had the number she gave me the night we met. One day God told me, "Call Juanita."

All those years passed and nothing happened for me with music. It hurt me. I didn't want Juanita to know how low I'd gone. When I got her on the phone, she remembered me and said, "I didn't think you wanted to talk to me." I didn't want to tell her I was living with my mother, but I did. She asked to come and see me, and I told her to, even though she had seen me one way and now I was another.

We got along great. She understood I needed to move on, and invited me to live with her family. The Lord coached me to go. I accepted. I had one set of raggedy underclothes. She cleaned me up and stitched my underclothes. She brought me to her church. I heard the women say, "What's he doing here? He plays the blues." Evidently, they'd been out to the clubs I had played in to know all that about me.

The pastor treated me kindly. He knew about my records. He made me feel welcome. Juanita took me to hear the gospel singing at an auditorium. I still had no job, but everything started going better. Another pastor, Rev. Higginbotham, used to go cut yards in the suburbs. He wasn't paying but $20-25. I asked if he could use me, and he took me along. We got paid and I gave the money to Juanita.

I always prayed I'd get to go play again. In 1983, Otis Clay took me to Japan for a ten-day tour. That helped for a minute. I came back with $2600. I was still in the same situation. Memphis was dead. Those days of the music had passed away. But Juanita and me stayed together. My high school bandleader, Mr. Able, felt concerned about my finances, and he knew I had Social Security due to me from all the records I cut. I didn't know anything about withholdings until he explained.

I still needed a job. I'd wanted to be a policeman since I was young. They always told me I was too slight. Now the best job I could get was to be a security guard. I started working but didn't carry a weapon. I had a stick and a dispatch radio, and just followed what God told me. I watched the training film three times to know what to do. I worked at a shopping center, at an office building, and a bank. I did that for about five, six years into the nineties.

One night I got off and drove to Hi Records. I went in and saw Willie Mitchell there. He looked like he was ready to go home. The place was full of hoes and thugs. Willie's grandson was partying up there. Willie saw me and thought I was police. I said no, just a man in uniform. He was gone from that liquor. He said, "Howard it's always good to see you."

I told Willie's grandson to take Willie home. I said that too
many people had worked hard to build this place and that man.
Willie's grandson begged my pardon. He went back in the studio
and cleaned the place out, sent everybody away. He got ready to take
Willie home. Before he left, Willie said to me, "This is your home.
You come here any time you want."

After that I felt more comfortable and spent more time at Hi
Records with Willie. One day, he told me I got a phone call at the
studio from Yoko Ono's agent. He said they wanted to put me on a
compilation of drummers. This happened in 1998.

I talked to the man, and he told me Bernard Purdie had recommended me—that's the greatest drummer we have. "Pretty" Purdie
recorded with James Brown and led the Aretha Franklin band.

The agent told me Yoko Ono would call me, and I spoke to
her the next day. She said she'd heard all of my work and that I play
great drums. She asked if I had any music of my own. I told her
about what I'd cut at Al Green's. She said she'd send $4000 for one
song. I got the check and went back over to Hi. Willie was so excited. He said, "Boy, you fittin' to go places."

I wanted to use the Hi Rhythm Section and the Memphis Horns.
Wayne Jackson and Andrew Love were about to go on tour and
couldn't make the session. I hired Lenny McMillan, Jack Hale, Scott
Thomas, and James Mitchell. They'd cut with the Memphis Horns,
but it didn't feel right to call them that without Wayne and Andrew.

Willie said to give the musicians $125 apiece. He said to get a
tape for the master recording that cost $125-150. He said to get it
set with the union, and give him $700 for the studio rent. Teenie
and them actually got mad and said, "You shouldn't charge Howard
nothing after all the records he cut. That ain't right." Willie took it
anyway. I had $1700 left after that. I put that in the bank.

Everybody was happy. Joy was in the studio that day. It felt like
it used to. Don Bryant came by. Ann Peebles came by. It was one of

the happiest days of my life. We cut my original song, called "Everybody's Music." It was the perfect title for getting us all back together. Willie said, "You got a smash!" James Mitchell did the charts.

During those slow years, I did my best to keep up with everybody from the glory days who'd stuck around Memphis.

My high school band director, Mr. Emerson Able, found me and told me, "Howard, I'm proud of you. You never gave up. All the shit people put you through, you stayed on your feet."

That gave me relief. I always wanted to impress Mr. Able and show him that his faith in me had proven true. As a teacher, he'd never tell you how good you were. We students didn't know what he thought of us. He said he didn't want anybody getting the big head. He said, "I stayed on you, because I knew how good you were. I didn't want you to get lazy." He made me understand I'd done well.

I found out that Isaac Hayes was staying in a penthouse suite at the Rivermont. I was rehearsing at that building one day. Getting my snare drum out of the station wagon, he pulled up. I called him by his name, but he didn't look up. I tried again and got nothing. So, I said, "Doom Broom," our old nickname for each other.

He said, "Howard, that you?" He came over and we got to chatting. I shared what had gone down with me. I gave him my spiritual testimony. He said, "Your time is coming. I'm gonna do something real good for you, because you deserve it. Howard, they done you wrong here." I don't know what he had in mind, but he never followed through on that promise.

Al Green remained good to me in many ways. After my mother took sick, I went to see her. She sat up in her hospital bed and just lit up. "Guess who came to see me?" she said. I asked who. She said, "Al Green! He came and he prayed with me!" She was so happy, I just didn't know what to say. He's hard to follow. Does some strange things and some very kind things. She felt so much better after that. My mother died in 2001. I think she would've stayed longer, but all of her friends had died and she felt lonely. All the joy she felt with her friends was behind her. She asked why she was still here. My mother said she wouldn't live to see my blessing. She didn't, but she's looking down.

My brother Dee Dee worked the streets. He went through a lot—prison. He got set up by guys he trusted. He pushed narcotics, that was his world. He made a lot of money and made other people a lot of money. That's the life he chose. He knew all of the top priority people. Everyone in that world spoke well of him, they'd say he's right on the money. He served two terms in prison, once for about ten years. He was kicking well during the late sixties, early seventies. I think people envied him because he didn't let anyone in on his business. He didn't give information.

That's also the reason everybody in the underworld respected him so. Pedro Lewis from a singing group called the Ovations lived in that world, too. He used to tell me, "Boy, Dee Dee Grimes is your brother, Howard? Dee Dee's straight, boy, everybody loved him." Playing music I never got into his field of work. One time he got busted, he had a partner that was working with him who turned out to be an undercover cop. He went through so much.

I worked a few times with Willie Mitchell after Hi Records was sold. We became better friends after that part of our relationship ended. I appreciated what a great artist he was after he'd stopped fucking me over on business. He always showed his appreciation for me and my work that had helped make him famous. He left me with one thing until today, and he lives on in the same way that all of the great musicians I've played with live in my heart after they've gone. Willie Mitchell gave me something that's allowed me to keep doing what I do. See, when we were cutting records back in the day, we never paid attention to lyrics. Willie Mitchell told me, "Listen to the story of the song. You'll know a hit record when you hear it."

After that, I hear the whole song. The process began with Al Green, the way every aspect of the song weaves together.

The story of my life has woven together with so many of the songs we recorded. But my years with Juanita have been happy and more settled than anything I felt while I was cutting hit records every day. We've stayed together longer than any record company I worked for.

Leroy Hodges, Otis Clay, Charles Hodges, Teenie Hodges, and me.
HOWARD GRIMES COLLECTION

Me with Charles, Teenie, Hubbie, and James Mitchell at Royal Studios, back together for the Yoko Ono project. HOWARD GRIMES COLLECTION

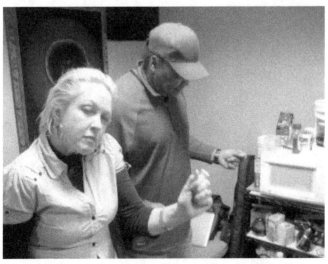

Cyndi Lauper and me keeping the beat at Electraphonic Studios.
COURTESY of SCOTT BOMAR

Me drumming at Royal Studios for the Yoko Ono project.
HOWARD GRIMES COLLECTION

Me with Skip Pitts. COURTESY of JACOB BLICKENSTAFF.

CHAPTER SEVENTEEN

I miss my friends who've gone on. I miss Andrew Love, I miss Wayne Jackson, I miss Willie, I miss everybody. Especially Darryl Carter. I think of all the great musicians I've known, who the world barely got to hear: James Austin, Benny Merl, Flukie. Time turns things around. When I came up, Bowlegs Miller and Ben Branch were hot. Their names are barely known today.

I still live in those old days, but I have new people in my life. Almost fifteen years ago, my high school bandleader, Mr. Able, told me, "There's a gentleman who's going to call you. I want you to take him everywhere and show him everything. He's the only real man to work with, because the rest of these motherfuckers ain't no good." My mouth had been closed all those years. Mr. Able thought very highly of Preston Lauterbach, and told me this was the man to tell the story to. So, here it is.

Preston and I have become real friends over the years. We go out to lunch and talk about old times I've had. That's how this book came together.

Just as I started getting to know Preston, a great music fan and writer named Red Kelly started to come to Memphis quite often from New York, and always came to see me. He said he'd been out to find O.V. Wright's gravesite, but that the grave had no marker. Red said it was a shame to bury O.V. like that. I didn't know where they'd buried him.

We discussed how O.V. deserved a tribute. The Hi Rhythm

Section never got the due that the artists at Stax received. All of us who'd been at Hi felt overlooked with all of the attention going to Stax. That O.V. tribute became the closest thing to a Hi tribute we ever got. The band got back together—me, Teenie, Charles, Leroy, and Hubbie—and we did the show at Morgan Freeman's club in Memphis in 2009.

Otis Clay came to sing O.V.'s songs. The Masqueraders did a few numbers. O.V.'s family came, including his son from Atlanta and the grandchildren O.V. never knew. Another of O.V.'s sons got on stage and sang just like his daddy.

The next day we laid a headstone on O.V.'s grave. I felt O.V.'s spirit go to rest.

The two members of Hi Rhythm that I've stayed close to are Leroy Hodges and Archie Turner, who we call Hubbie.

Leroy and I have played in juke joints and Beale Street clubs with guitarist Little Jimmy King and Jesse Dotson, a keyboard player who used to lead Albert King's band. Any time the Hi Rhythm Section gets a gig—we've played the Ponderosa Stomp in New Orleans for a great crowd—Leroy and I room together, and we make sure to eat our share in the green room.

Hubbie has had me up to play at a juke joint called Wild Bill's over the years. He's the one who gave my recording career a new life. In 2010, Hubbie brought me to Electraphonic Recording studios in Memphis and introduced me to Scott Bomar.

Scott formed a group of soul musicians, those who were left from Stax and Hi, and called them the Bo-Keys. Over the years, he's had trumpeter Ben Cauley of the Bar-Kays, and guitarist Skip Pitts, from Isaac Hayes's band, in the group. They've backed up Percy Wiggins, a great vocalist who recorded in the '60s, and my old Hi Records colleague Don Bryant, plus William Bell from Stax.

Scott also has great young soul men working with him, horn players Jim Spake, Art Edmaiston, and Marc Franklin, guitarist Joe Restivo. Scott plays a good bass.

Some of what we do with Scott is cut outside artists who come to the studio. My first record was with Cyndi Lauper, who did that song about girls always having a good time. She came to us to cut her *Memphis Blues* album.

Cyndi brought in some great partners to cut duets with. I had to tell Allen Toussaint not to run. He got on that piano and lost all track of the beat. I stopped the song and laid it down. I said, "I'm the timekeeper. I'm here to keep y'all in place."

I grew up with Allen Toussaint's music, so it felt strange to stop him, but I had to. He ran off with the time. That's my department, my responsibility. I can't let anybody take the time.

I'm not angry with Stax. I'm not angry with Hi. But Scott Bomar at Electraphonic is the only person who's ever paid me right. I was shocked when he paid me for the session on Cyndi Lauper. He said I deserve it.

Working with Scott is almost like being back with Willie Mitchell. Electraphonic is the only place left that feels like the glory days.

The world of today isn't the place I knew coming up. The joy, the fun, the safety, are all gone. Memphis, Tennessee turned rotten. During my early years, the streets were under control. In the twenty-first century, everyone's gone nuts. My friend Willie Wine tells me, "Lucifer got 'em." I'm not around happy people now. I'm around people that believe in the gun. I'm around hoes in my neighborhood. I ain't happy to know them. It's been darkness around Memphis. People love darkness.

I love light, I don't like darkness. I've seen enough darkness. I saw the devil, twice. He talked to me. The first time I ran into the devil he was a tall motherfucker in a black suit with bloodshot eyes.

His voice roared. "What's your name?"

I said, "Motherfucker, what's your name?" He didn't say any more.

141

Second time, I saw him at three o' clock in the morning. It was wintertime. He had on a long coat. I nearly ran over him with my car. He walked along like a hunchback. I told him to get out of the way before he gets himself killed. He raised up on me and I saw he had a demon face. I drove past and when I looked for him in my rearview, he'd gone. I've seen enough of the devil in my lifetime.

Things people got in later years, they had through me. I'm the one who cut gold records and put money in their pockets. I rode on the back of those raggedy trucks for politicians. They couldn't draw a fly without musicians. I worked to make everybody else rich. When it was time for me to get something, I got nothing. I used to worry about that.

It took me until my seventies to understand God's plan. It ain't to have houses and cars. It's to live. People said I had no sense. I've seen them all come and go, the clowns. I never sinned. I'm kept at peace. I don't care how you test me, you ain't gonna find nothing on me. You're gonna find the life of Christ in me.

I saw music bring this city to life. Wasn't anything happening in Memphis before. Not much has happened since it died down. Hip hop ain't it. The young people take our hard work and make money off of it, but can't play like we did. There's no educational value in what they do, no uplift. The message is violence and anger. It ain't love and happiness. People still come to the city from all over the world to see what was.

When Elvis lifted Memphis music, we already had so much to work with. Nightclubs were full of talent. The schools developed talent. The fans wanted to come out and hear the best. That already existed before the big business side of things happened. Elvis's hit records inspired studios to open up. Those studios found their own sounds, and made their own artists. The money and success that followed ended up being bad for the music. Greed, corruption, and violence killed us. It killed Al Jackson Jr. It killed Stax. It killed Hi Records. If we could have stayed on peace and togetherness, we'd still be on top.

I believe in my city and always will. We still have the creativity and the character we had in those days. I walk these streets of Memphis with my faith. I want to be a big help to this city. I saw how it developed. My mother used to say, "All that's old will be new again." This city's music has to be reborn. The Memphis sound will return. When it does, my time will come again. That's my dream.

THE END

Howard Grimes, born in 1941, played drums on the first hit records at Stax Records and the major hits at Hi Records, making him a cornerstone of the Memphis sound.

Preston Lauterbach, born in 1974, is author of *The Chitlin' Circuit, Beale Street Dynasty,* and *Bluff City,* and co-author of *Brother Robert,* making him a big fan of the Memphis sound.

ACKNOWLEDGMENTS

Thanks to so many great friends for making this book possible: John Riley and Maryellen Riley, in memory of George Riley, Tom Graves, Kerri Mahoney, Scott Bomar, Harry Duncan, Red Kelly, Bruce Bramoweth, and Robin Tomlin. Thanks also to the many friends who have gone on, but made this history happen.

Other Books in

THE GREAT MUSIC BOOK SERIES

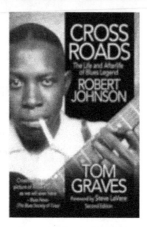

Crossroads: The Life and Afterlife of Blues Legend Robert Johnson by **Tom Graves**

This second edition of the award-winning *Crossroads* by Tom Graves is the author-approved new manuscript that contains updated information and new photographs related to blues legend Robert Johnson. *Crossroads* won the Keeping the Blues Alive Award in Literature in 2010 from the prestigious Blues Foundation and is considered the definitive word on its enigmatic subject.

The result of careful and meticulous research, this stylishly-written biography of infamous blues musician Robert Johnson reveals the real story behind the mythical talent that made him a musical legend. Available in print, ebook, and audiobook, read by the author himself.

Sun Records: An Oral History by John Floyd

Rock 'n' roll was created in tiny Sun Records in Memphis, Tennessee, by owner Sam Phillips, who introduced the world to Elvis, Johnny Cash, Jerry Lee Lewis, Rufus Thomas, Carl Perkins, and many others. Brush up on your knowledge of Sun's legendary performers by purchasing a copy of *Sun Records: An Oral History* from DevaultGraves Books.

You'll be treated to the voices of the pillars of Sun, the artists, producers and engineers who made the place tick.

Sun Records: An Oral History by author John Floyd is available in print and ebook formats.

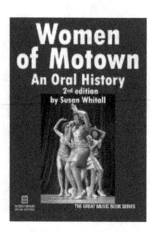

Women of Motown: An Oral History by Susan Whitall

The second edition of *Women of Motown* by author Susan Whitall contains new chapters and information, updating this critically-acclaimed oral history of the ladies who made Motown a sound heard round the world. Originally published to glowing reviews in 1998, the first edition has long been out of print and sought after by collectors. Devault Graves Books now brings the public a new updated edition that tells the Motown story from its beginnings with Mable John through the great girl groups such as Martha and the Vandellas and ending with the last iteration of the glorious Supremes after Diana Ross left for superstar status. Author Susan Whitall, an esteemed music writer who is a native of Detroit, expertly interviewed virtually all the women who made Motown explode on the hit charts and lets them tell their stories in all their humor, dishy detail, and the glory of lives spent recording and singing some of the greatest songs ever written.

Fans of Motown will not want to miss this chance for the girls to let their hair down and lay it on the line. The stories are not only fun and exciting, but give a history of a remarkable company that took African American music from Detroit's housing projects to the White House.

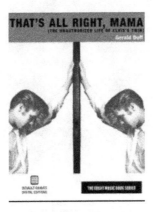

That's All Right, Mama by Gerald Duff

Did Elvis' identical twin, Jesse Garon Presley, really die at birth?
Not according to Lance Lee, the hero of Gerald Duff's darkly comic
dissection of fame and rock 'n' roll.

Lee, who makes his living as an Elvis imitator, claims to be the
long-presumed dead twin. In a style that faithfully reproduces Elvis'
plaintive bravado, Lance-Jesse recounts being hidden away and
passed off as Elvis' "cousin" until he needs to impersonate Elvis to
stave off bullies at school; later, he is obliged to "play Elvis" every
time The King has an attack of nerves.

As performing substitute, Jesse has had a lifetime to enjoy being a
good-timing, honey-loving, non-drug-dependent Elvis.

DEVAULT
GRAVES
BOOKS